Latina/o y Musulmán

LATINA/O Y MUSULMÁN
The Construction of Latina/o Identity among Latina/o Muslims in the United States

Pickwick Publications
An Imprint of Wipf and Stock Publishers
199 W. 8th Ave., Suite 3
Eugene, OR 97401

www.wipfandstock.com

Portions of this book have been published, in different format, in Hjamil A. Martínez-Vázquez, "Finding Enlightenment: U.S. Latina/o's Journey to Islam," *Journal of Latino-Latin American Studies* 3, no. 2 (Winter 2008), 57–71 [reprinted by permission]; and Hjamil A. Martínez-Vázquez, "Conversion and the Re-construction of Identity: The Case of U.S. Latina/o Muslims," *Apuntes* (Fall 2009)[reprinted by permission].

ISBN 13: 978-1-60899-0900

Cataloging-in-Publication data:

Martínez-Vázquez, Hjamil A.

Latina/o y Musulmán : the construction of Latina/o identity among Latina/o Muslims in the United States / Hjamil A. Martínez-Vázquez.

x + 150 p. ; 23 cm. — Includes bibliographical references and index.

isbn 13: 978-1-60899-0900

1. Latin Americans—Religion. 2. Hispanic Americans—Religion. 3. Muslims—United States. I. Title.

BR563.H57 M35 2010

Manufactured in the U.S.A.

Latina/o y Musulmán

*The Construction of Latina/o Identity
among Latina/o Muslims in the United States*

Hjamil A. Martínez-Vázquez

PICKWICK *Publications* · Eugene, Oregon

Para mi madre, Edda Vázquez

Mi primer y mejor ejemplo

Contents

Acknowledgments

MANY DIFFERENT INDIVIDUALS ARE responsible for the publication of this work, which has taken many years to come to fruition. First, I have to acknowledge the individuals from the U.S. Latina/o Muslim community who accepted the invitation to participate in this project. Without them, this project would still be an idea. Especially, I owe thanks to the particular people who put the different groups together in the four different cities and to Juan Galván, executive director of LADO, whose support allowed me to find some credibility within the community. At the same time, without the help of an RCAF grant from Texas Christian University and a Junior Scholar Grant by the Southwest Commission on Religious Studies, I would have never been able to conduct the research to complete this project.

Saddyna Belmashkan worked on the transcription of the interviews and as a U.S. Latina Muslim herself brought some suggestions and critiques to the initial part of the project. Samantha Bennett also helped with the transcription and put together many of the bibliographical material. This manuscript has gone through multiple revisions and I am thankful to the mentors, friends and colleagues who reviewed the previous versions and with keen eye provided thoughtful and critical suggestions in order to improve the final product. Manuel Vásquez, Alberto Pulido, and Darren Middleton pushed me to further my argument. In the same way, U.S. Latino Muslims Juan Galván and Justin Mauro Benavidez after reading my work challenged me to see beyond the academic lingo into the real experiences of the people. I hope this final product reflects my sincere intention to put the experience of the people at the front of this work. But I would have never been able to put all the ideas together without the work of Ulrike Guthrie, the best editor in the world.

Finally, I want to thank some people whose support and inspiration have made this book possible. I am indebted to David Daniels, Arlene Sánchez-Walsh, Sean McMillan, and Eliseo Pérez for their constant

Acknowledgments

acompañamiento and the spaces of trust they provide. In addition, I am thankful to my brothers and sister and their families: Omar Martínez-Vázquez, Edgardo Martínez-Vázquez, Isabel Martínez-Torres, Kalitza Baerga, Monica Rivera, Omar Ignacio, Gustavo Andrés, and Alma Zoé. To my father, Edgardo Martínez-Nazario, and my mother, Edda Vázquez-Beitía, I owe the education and confidence that allowed me to get to this point. Finally, most important, I am grateful for the unconditional love and presence of my wife Vanessa González-López and our son Estéfano Martínez-Gónzalez.

Introduction

Understanding the Matter

"ARE YOU SAYING THAT I am less Puerto Rican than you because I am not Catholic?"

I was responding to my ninth-grade religion teacher's statement that: "[H]ere [in Puerto Rico], Protestants are less nationalistic, or even less Puerto Rican, than Catholics." And so began a long debate between us over religion's role in identity construction and formation. My teacher argued that since Protestantism "was brought" to the island by U.S. Americans after the invasion of 1898, becoming Protestant was a symbol of Americanization and not of Latin American identity. She believed that the Catholic faith was an intrinsic aspect of Latin American identity and, for that matter, of our *puertorriqueñidad* (Puerto Rican identity) because of the legacy of Spanish Catholicism's domination in the Americas. Of course this debate was not resolved in our fifty-minute class that day and, while this example focuses on the Puerto Rican case, it reflects a broader assumption that Christianity—specifically, Roman Catholicism—plays a primary role in the construction of identities among Latin Americans.

A couple of years ago, I was reminded of that debate with my teacher when a puzzled college student in my course on Latina/o Religions in the United States asked, "Aren't all Hispanics Catholic?" It was clear that though the Protestant/Pentecostal presence in Latin America is significant, the traditional stereotype of Latin Americans being Catholics survives, especially in the United States. It is true that most U.S. Latina/os have a Roman Catholic background. However, with the growth of U.S. Latina/o Pentecostal churches and other independent Christian movements, new generations of U.S. Latina/os are increasingly tracing their religious identity to a non-Catholic Christian heritage.[1] "The fact of the

---

1. In this book I will use U.S. Latina/o to refer to the people of Latin American

1

matter is," I explained to my student, "that U.S. Latina/o religious identities for the most part have been based upon a Christian paradigm, whether Catholic or Protestant." Yet not all Latina/os in the U.S. are Christian. For example, there are growing numbers of U.S. Latina/o Muslims and it is they who are the focus of this book. Religion and religious experiences turn out to be foundational in the understanding of identity construction for Latin Americans and U.S. Latina/os. Because many communities turn to their religious experiences as a source for their cultural memories, it is important to understand how this dynamic works not only for the Christian majority, but also for religious minorities.

U.S. Latina/o Muslims constitute a group in its nascent stages; they are only beginning to construct their identities, as both U.S. Latina/o and Muslim. While the American Muslim Council estimated that in 1997 there were 40,000 Latina/o Muslims in the United States, and while as recently as 2006, Ali Khan, national director of the American Muslim Council in Chicago, claimed that this number had increased five-fold to 200,000, most current conservative estimates suggest that the U.S. Latina/o Muslim population is somewhere between 50,000 and 75,000. Not surprisingly, the densest populations of U.S. Latina/o Muslims can be found in cities with higher U.S. Latino populations, like New York, Chicago, and Los Angeles. Though there are a number of U.S. Latina/o Muslims who were born into Islam, for the most part this community is made up of converts, most of whom are female. Juan Galván, executive director of the Latino American Da'wah Organization (LADO), describes this community as follows:

> Interestingly, Latinas are more willing to convert than Latinos, many of whom are too afraid to change. According to Samantha Sanchez's research, most converts are college-educated, between the ages of 20 and 30, and female. By far, the vast majority of Latino Muslims are Sunni. According to LADO's ongoing SLM project, most Latino Muslims are married and have more than one child. As is true of most Latino families, Latino Muslim families are traditionally larger than their American counterparts, which helps

---

descent living in the United States. I will not use the term "America" to refer to the United States since it is a concept imbued with imperialism and ethnocentrism that silences the rest of the Americas; likewise, I do not use the term "American" without the prefix U.S., to refer to the people from the United States.

explain the community's rapid growth. It is not only about individuals converting; it is about entire families embracing Islam.[2]

Because of the lack of numbers and census data, it is impossible to actually grasp the growth of this community, but it should not be surprising
that U.S. Latina/os, the fastest growing minoritized group in the United
States, is finding Islam, one of the fastest growing religions in the country. As we explore in this book, reasons for conversion vary even if the
underlying disenchantment with Christianity appears to be present in
most narratives of conversion. But, what becomes clear is that, after they
convert, U.S. Latina/o Muslims are forced to re-construct their identities
and re-define the normative understandings of U.S. Latina/o identities,
which become inadequate to them after their conversion.

While U.S. Latina/o converts to Islam are by no means a homogeneous group, they do share common conditions of isolation after their
conversion, both within their own ethnic/racial group as well as within
the broader society. In some cases, they are considered "less" U.S. Latina/
os by some members of the larger U.S. Latino community and "not necessarily" as good Muslims by members of the larger U.S. Muslim community. In the first case, the attitude represents the belief that Christianity
(especially Catholicism) is an intrinsic aspect of U.S. Latina/o identities.
The latter represents the belief by some members of the Muslim community in the United States that U.S. Latina/o [false] stereotypes, such as a
purported adulterous and drunken nature, prevent them from becoming
good Muslims. In this regards, the decision of conversion situates U.S.
Latina/o Muslims in a liminal or in-between space. They are members
of both communities while yet encountering isolation within both. As a
response, they create organizations, albeit sometimes virtually, allowing
them to build and become part of a community that offers nourishment
and a sense of belonging. Participation in these organizations and/or the
opportunity to share stories and experiences offer U.S. Latina/o Muslims
the prospect of not only exploring and making sense of their decision but
also or re-defining their identities as a group.

This process of identity re-construction is established as U.S.
Latina/o Muslims engage in an act of remembering. This remembering
takes place as U.S. Latina/o Muslims "go back" and investigate the historical narratives in order to re-construct their historical consciousness.

2. Galván, "Who are Latino Muslims?," 29.

The re-construction of this consciousness occurs in dis-covering cultural memory through religious experience.[3] This dis-covery points to the fact that the act of remembering is not only an individual and social activity; it also incorporates a cultural aspect which in turns adds a dimension of "lived experience" to the representations of the past, much like a ritual does. Through the use of cultural memory, history is no longer a narrative of the past in a vacuum, but a link between the past and the present. This means that people look at themselves as part of a history while focusing on "passing on" (or transmitting) that history, those memories, to other members of their family or community. To achieve the re-construction, they look at the history of Muslim Spain as the source of those dis-covered cultural memories that serve the process of identity construction. As reporter Lisa Viscidi finds, "Many Latinos who convert to Islam believe they are reclaiming their lost Muslim and African heritage—which they view more positively than the legacy of Catholicism."[4] This recovery of the "silenced" past regarding Muslim Spain challenges both of the attitudes that place U.S. Latina/o Muslims in a liminal space by arguing, through a new historical consciousness, that there is nothing disconnected about being Latina/o and Muslim. On the contrary, this historical consciousness suggests that the two are historical and culturally intertwined.

The condition of liminality opens the door for this act of remembering through which a particular community can either attempt to assimilate into the mainstream or dis-cover a cultural memory to serve in the construction of identities different from that established as normative by the mainstream. This decision—to assimilate or to resist—determines the way members of the community see and re-interpret representations of the past: either following traditional histories that leave them without a voice, or confronting those histories with new interpretations that allow new voices into the historical discourses. In the case of U.S. Latina/o Muslims, the decision to convert already implies a rejection of the normative narratives for the re-construction of new ones. These new interpreta-

---

3. As I have stated elsewhere concerning "dis-covery": "It serves the marginal, the subaltern, in the quest for an identity, a self-identity, different from that which has been placed upon her/him by the people who covered up the memory. It is a way of breaking away from the colonial heritage imposed on knowledge." [Martínez-Vázquez, *Dis*-covering the Silences," 55.] Thus, I use "dis-covery" here to suggest a process of un-covering that which has been covered up by history and by those in power.

4. Viscidi, "Latino Muslims," para. 9.

tions, available through the act of remembering, allow those outside of the mainstream to transform their condition of being objects of history and instead become historical subjects. Acquiring this subjectivity implies that one is able to be in charge of constructing one's own identity rather than being "constructed" by someone else. Thus, one is in charge of interpreting the past and remembering from one's own social location. Remembering becomes a process of reshaping the community's past. Recovering a cultural memory can thus lead to new perceptions of identities. Following theologian Jeanette Rodríguez and anthropologist Ted Fortier, I understand cultural memory as "transmit[ting] an experience rooted in history that has reached a culturally definitive, potentially transformative status."[5] This transformative status happens when individuals recover the stories that have been hidden by the official history imposed by those in power, and when they use these voices as a key source in the process of their identity construction. Identity construction, as the act of remembering, needs to be understood as a process that evolves; it is never fixed but is always being transformed. Religious experiences inform this process through the act of cultural memory because through these experiences, U.S. Latina/os create connections between the present condition and the past, connection that heretofore have been hidden. This applies to U.S Latina/o Christians and U.S. Latina/o Muslims alike, even though their respective "experiences rooted in history" may be different. But, it is important to acknowledge that the identities re-constructed by U.S. Latina/o Muslims challenge those of the U.S. Latina/o Christians that has become the norm. At the same time, these new perspectives challenge the academic religious discourses about U.S. Latina/os that have been constructed within a Christian paradigm.

RESEARCH

After September 11, 2001, many in the United States became openly suspicious of Muslims, even if they were neighbors, co-workers, or long-time friends. Reported and unreported hate crimes escalated against Muslims all across the United States, exacerbated by the government's "legal" witch-hunt through the establishment of the Patriot Act. Many U.S. Muslims were detained for no particular reason other than their name, religion, and/or country of origin. I was often stopped at airport security two or

5. Rodríguez and Fortier, *Cultural Memory*, 12.

three times per trip for so-called "random" security checks. I have never been Muslim, but I have an Arabic name and a Latino surname, so it did not take me much time to realize what was going on.

These experiences made me realize the validity of the "rumors" that there was a sizeable and growing Latina/o Muslim community in the United States. What puzzled me was why somebody who is already marginalized by mainstream society would convert to a religion that will only increase that marginalization, even to the point of persecution? I decided to investigate. Finding materials was not always easy because, as Juan Galván states, "Most information on Latino Muslims comes from Latino Muslim organizations instead of academia, which has essentially ignored them."[6] So, I started searching online for stories or websites about U.S. Latina/o Muslims, and to my surprise found copious amounts of information regarding this community, information that has more than tripled in the last four years. As I started my research, the FBI announced the arrest of José Padilla, a Puerto Rican convert to Islam, on suspicion of terrorist activities.[7] This arrest put the case of U.S. Latina/o Muslims front and center in my life, and what had been simply an item of curiosity to me became a two-year long research activity.

After these two years of reading materials on the Internet and talking to multiple acquaintances, I decided to officially begin making contacts within the U.S. Latina/o Muslim community in order to be able to inter-view them. This process turned out to be harder than I expected because of the resistance to outsiders of groups within this community. The con-stant harassment of the U.S. government and the aggressive proselytizing activities of Christian churches has led to many U.S. Latina/o Muslims developing a well-founded mistrust of people who want to know more about their situation. This mistrust led many to reject my initial requests, even to the point of that some started to ask and even warn friends not to participate in the project because of my supposed intentions. The fact that the name of my institution includes not only the word Texas but also Christian, heightened their mistrust.[8] Some phone and email attacks

6. Galván, 30.

7. An analysis of his arrest and (much later) conviction lies beyond the scope of this book.

8. Weeks after I started contacting the leaders of the different Latina/o Muslims orga-nizations across the United States to ask for their help in the development of my research project, I received an email from a member of the community warning me that an email

on me were indeed frustrating, but mitigated by my own experiences of being stopped at airport security checkpoints. It took months, and it took lots of conversations by email and phone, but after much work, I finally was able to make enough contacts with members of U.S. Latina/o Muslim groups to be able to arrange some interviews as part of my project.[9]

During the summer of 2006, with the support of a grant from the Research and Creative Activities Fund at Texas Christian University, I was then also able to visit the U.S. Latina/o Muslims groups in New York, Chicago, Los Angeles, and San Francisco. I interviewed twenty people in total, not including others with whom I established contact through email. I began my journey in New York, where I interviewed a U.S. Latina Muslim in a Starbucks near Madison Square Gardens.[10] From there I traveled to Chicago, and interviewed a group of seven U.S. Latinas who had converted to Islam and were active participants in a Spanish-speaking study group for Latinas. This study group was organized and led by my initial contact in the city. In Los Angeles, I met with a group of six U.S. Latina/o Muslims, which was put together by two contacts in the area outside the city. I then traveled north to San Francisco and met with six members of the Latino Muslims Association of the Bay Area.

Except for my interview with María in New York, all the interviews were conducted in a group setting, where individuals were able not only to tell their conversion story and answer my questions but also able to respond to one another's stories and experiences. I focused our conversa-

---

has been sent out to other members asking them not to participate in my research. The email, as it was forwarded to me, read: "I have received more than one time a message from H. Martinez-Vazquez, who is doing a research study about Latinos/as converting to Islam. This professor works for an Ultra Christian University in Texas. LALMA has declined to participate in this research study. We believe that the information gather from this research will be used against us in the future. The following is a sample of his proposal; if you are interested I will e-mail you the entire proposal. Please, investigate this person and the type of University where he teaches, and warn our brothers and sisters not to participate in this research study. I just wander, Why a Christian University will be so interested in learning about Latino/as converts?" It is important to establish that once I was able to contact some individuals to participate in the project, this same person tried to prevent them from participation.

9. In order to maintain confidentiality, I will use pseudonyms to refer to individuals interviewed for this book.

10. I was scheduled to interview a group of U.S. Latina/o Muslims from the New York/New Jersey area but three days before the actual trip that plan fell apart because of what I was told by my contact were scheduling issues.

tions on their conversion stories and the reasons behind those decisions while also trying to get a sense of how they see themselves within the larger U.S. Latino community. The conversations were divided into three major parts: 1) conversion, 2) responses to conversion, and 3) perception of U.S. Latina/o identities in light of new religious experience. In the first part, the individuals narrated their conversion stories. In the second, they addressed the responses of their family and friends to their conversions. Finally, I asked them to share their perceptions about U.S. Latina/o identities now that they did not fit the traditional stereotype of U.S. Latina/os as being Catholics (or at least Christian).[11] These conversations gave me a better understanding of how conversion for them is a process rather than a one-time event and how this process allows a move toward a re-construction of their U.S. Latina/o identities. Each of them still remembers when they had taken the *shahadah*—the initial ritual entry into Islam; but as they told it, their conversions were not limited to this specific event or end result.

Based on their stories, the pages that follow examine how conversion triggers a move toward the re-construction of identities by U.S. Latina/o Muslims. Given the absence of major academic research exploring U.S. Latina/o Muslims, these Muslims' voices have been mostly absent from discussions about U.S. Latina/o identities. Magazine articles have explored the social location of U.S. Latina/o Muslims within the larger Muslim community, but this is the first book formally to research the ways in which Muslims construct their U.S. Latina/o identities. Furthermore, since Latina/o religious experiences in the United States up until now have largely assumed Christianity as the *de facto* religion, this work brings a fresh perspective to studies in this area.

In order to read and interpret these narratives and grasp the movement toward new identities, I use the lenses of postcolonial criticism, postcolonialism offering an illuminating subaltern perspective on how U.S. Latina/o Muslims struggle to challenge the construction of the normative understandings of identities. In this sense, as they are located in a liminal space, their conversion stories represent counter-discourses and the process toward the re-construction of identities as a decolonial activity.

---

11. For time constraints I was not able to have this part of the discussion with the group in Chicago, as the other two parts took longer than the time we had together.

SOCIAL LOCATION AND AGENDA OF THE BOOK

An author's particular social location and agenda necessarily shapes his research. I am no exception. So where am I coming from? What is my agenda? I believe that no academic project of deconstruction or construction should be understood as objective, but rather as localized within a particular perspective and within a particular agenda. I want to be as self-reflective as possible in creating a discourse that challenges the authority of traditional paradigms that fix categories by assigning them one meaning or by assuming a particular unity and linearity of the past.[12]

I am not a member of the U.S. Latina/o Muslim community, and for that reason this book is written from the perspective of an outsider. Moreover, while those in the larger U.S. society consider me a U.S. Latino, I see myself as a participant-outsider of that reality because of my heritage as a Puerto Rican who did not migrate to the United States until his mid-twenties. I understand that Latina/o Muslims in the United States are in the process of developing particular identities located within two different worlds, Latina/o and Muslim, while being situated in liminal spaces within both. In this book, I focus my analysis exclusively on the way conversion to Islam affects U.S. Latina/o Muslims in their process of reconstructing their U.S. Latino/a identities. While I make some references to the larger Muslim community in the United States, I do not target the core of my analysis to the issues that U.S. Latina/o Muslims confront within that larger community, so I will not enter into a discussion about the core aspects of Islam.

This book is an invitation to rethink how we understand the U.S. Latina/o community and the way identities are constructed to take into account the key role religious experiences play within this process. I challenge stereotypical perspectives about U.S. Latina/o identities, especially regarding religion, while at the same time confronting the way our academic disciplines—such as U.S. Latina/o religious studies—seem to have forgotten about the multiplicity of religious experiences within the community and have focused only on Christian experiences. When U.S. Latina/o Muslims are kept outside of academic discourses their stories are silenced. The absence of their voices leaves them outside of the broader community's history and without an articulated and shared historical memory.

12. Scott, *Gender*, 8.

This nullification of U.S. Latina/o Muslim experience reflects the way colonial discourses work—that is, by erasing the memory of the colonized. Such discourses need to be deconstructed in order to interrupt domination by those who want to maintain power through a system where they, as the "winners," get to write history and define everybody else. I call this system a colonial imaginary, "a framework, a set of ideological strategies of containment by which everything is explained and organized, ensuring thereby the consensus of the dominated and their consent to their domination."[13] By including these new voices of previously "unknown" and/or silenced people—in this case, U.S. Latina/o Muslims—we open our theories to new perspectives and develop more just systems of analysis and understanding, which can then help in the construction of a decolonial imaginary.[14] The process of re-construction of identity after conversion, which entails confrontation of the established imaginary, serves as an example of an activity that I interpret as subversion of the colonial imaginary. This decolonial imaginary is a framework filled with ideologies, perspectives, and histories that ensure social justice and liberation.[15]

To understand the way U.S. Latina/o Muslims dis-cover their cultural memory in order to construct their identities in the face of colonizing dominant narratives, we need to use a paradigm that deconstructs the colonial aspects of identity construction and illuminates new non-colonial approaches to this process. I call this paradigm a postcolonizing project.[16]

13. Sánchez, "The history of Chicanas," 4.

14. Here, I make an effort to identify U.S. Latina/o Muslim's voices not only as being unknown but also as being silenced. I recognized that in many cases these voices have not been heard because the data available is minor, but since the normative discourses have only focused on Christian narratives, there has been no particular concern to actually uncover them. Thus, they become silenced voices. On the other hand, for a discussion on imaginary see Martínez-Vázquez, "Shifting the Discursive Space."

15. While political, social, religious and economic leaders based their actions in the existing colonial imaginary (manifest destiny, racism, heterosexism, classicism, misogyny, and economic and cultural dominance of the North Atlantic empire), the development of a decolonial imaginary destroys this existing imaginary and the major consequence is that people would leave behind oppression and search for social justice. Social justice and liberation should be the overarching schemes of this decolonial imaginary so it can bring about change in society.

16. I prefer the term postcolonizing over the terms postcolonial and anti-colonial. Postcolonialism is an ongoing process. I agree with Ato Quayson, who talks about postcolonizing instead of postcolonialism. [See Quayson, Postcolonialism]. But using the term

This project uses the tools provided by the disciplines of cultural studies, postcolonial studies, and historical studies to develop a framework through which one can understand the development of identities among marginalized groups. Since U.S. Latina/os live in the midst of liminality, it is important to analyze how that condition of being seen as Other informs their process of identity construction, and how religious experience enhances our understanding of the process. I use this postcolonizing project to analyze the re-construction of identities among U.S. Latina/o Muslims.

STRUCTURE OF THE BOOK

The process of conversion by U.S. Latina/o Muslims cannot be understood outside of the socio-cultural contexts of the individuals. These contexts determine the reasons for conversion and the consequences of that decision. Hence, the first two chapters of the book introduce and examine the process of conversion in the multiple contexts. The second two chapters offer an analysis of the way that after conversion there is a process of re-construction of identity, and how this process challenges the normative understandings of U.S. Latina/o identities.

In the first chapter, I discuss how Latina/o Muslims establish themselves and make their presence felt in the United States. I introduce the importance of conversion narratives in the process of understanding this community. These conversion narratives should be understood as spiritual life stories, which help us locate this community. They way individuals "put together" these stories hints at the importance of the act of remembering as a subversive practice. In order to offer the reader a chance of better comprehending this community, I include eight of the conversion narratives that I gathered from my research.

"postcolonizing," I am arguing that people who are no longer politically colonized but have adopted or internalized the imperial discourses also need to immerse themselves in the process of postcolonization. I prefer postcolonizing over the terms postcolonial and anti-colonial because postcolonizing implies a movement towards a goal, which entails the re-creation of one's past and the re-construction of an identity. In the same sense, it is important to explain my use of the terms "postcolonizing," and "decolonial." The first term implies a movement from coloniality to decolonialism. My use of the term implies that I visualize this enterprise as an ongoing process, not a finished one. The term "decolonial" implies the already-attained end of colonialism. Here, "decolonial" will only be associated with the imaginary that it is formed after the different postcolonizing projects have built it.

In chapter 2, I examine the stories of conversion by U.S. Latina/o Muslims, and their social location once they make that decision. Here, I analyze their reasons for conversion and the ways in which they re-construct their lives, customs, and traditions (such as food and prayer) in light of their newfound religion. Through their stories and experiences we see that U.S. Latina/o Muslims confront some isolation within their communities and that this pushes them into a condition of liminality among their own people. To assuage this sense of liminality, U.S. Latina/o Muslims gather in local and virtual organizations where they build new communities and through which they begin to make sense of their deci-sion and their condition of being in-between.

In the third chapter, I continue my analysis of the effects of conver-sion among U.S. Latina/o Muslims and how their new religious experi-ence informs identity re-construction. Most U.S. Latina/o Muslims speak of reversion instead of conversion because they see themselves as "going back" to an original state, not "converting" to anything. The process of reversion becomes a catalyst for their dis-covering a cultural memory, which they see as their historical and religious heritage. In their construc-tion of new identities, they retrieve their Moorish Spanish identity. While this dis-covered cultural memory challenges the Christian paradigm that has dominated traditional and common understandings of U.S. Latina/o identities, U.S. Latina/o Muslims do not see themselves as being separate from this community. On the contrary, by focusing the construction of identities on this cultural memory, they see themselves as an integral part of the U.S. Latina/o community.

I begin the fourth and final chapter by examining the traditional ways U.S. Latina/o identities have been categorized in order to understand how we might re-define the ways we have understood Latina/o identities in the United States by more fully taking into account religious experience. After this discussion I compare and contrast the way U.S. Latina/o Muslims use cultural memory as a vehicle with the way two other U.S. Latina/o groups also use cultural memory as way of building up their identities: the sym-bol of the social martyrs among Salvadorans, and Our Lady of Charity among Cubans in Miami. Even when there are differences, this analysis allows us to understand that U.S. Latina/o Muslims' re-construction of identities should not be seen apart from the way most U.S. Latina/os use religious experience in the same identity construction process. My intent is not to develop a definitive analysis of the way U.S. Latina/o Muslims use cultural and historical memory to construct their identities. Rather, I offer the re-constructed historical consciousness to Latina/o scholars and other U.S. scholars as one aspect that needs to be included within the new analyses regarding identities. As an example, I deconstruct the way U.S. Latina/o scholars in religion have been using the concept of *mestizaje* and how the historical consciousness provided by U.S. Latina/o Muslims brings new challenges to its normative understanding by the inclusion of the Muslim past. This serves as a call to these and other scholars to take seriously the presence of this community and how it benefits our own identities.

Telling the Story of U.S. Latina/o Muslim Experience

THE HISTORY OF THE Latina/o Muslim in the United States, while always related to the movement of Spanish Muslims (Moors) to the Americas during the colonization and conquest, cannot be traced to a particular historical event. It would be hard to establish a linear history that cleanly connects the events of the conquest and colonization of the Americas and the development of Latina/o Muslims communities all over the United States. This attempt is even harder as most of the history regarding Muslims in the Americas during the Spanish and Portuguese colonization has been marginalized and sometimes even silenced. Thus, in order to understand the present condition of the U.S. Latina/o Muslim community and its growth in the past decade, one cannot look into a single factor but rather consider this growth as the result of multiple conditions and situations over the course of time. Khalil Al-Puerto Rikani in his article focusing on the Puerto Rican community in New York entitled "Latino Conversion to Islam: From African-American/Latino Neighbors to Muslim/Latino Global Neighbors," finds that there are five different ways U.S. Latina/os come to Islam: (1) Puerto Rican/African-American interactions; (2) the Internet; (3) Latinos living among immigrant Muslims; (4) prisons; and (5) marriage.[1] He suggests that together these five ways explain growth of the U.S. Latino Muslim community.[2]

The first way is intrinsically related to the relationship between the Latino community and the African American community in the United

---

1. Rikani, "Latino Conversion to Islam," para. 3.

2. Rikani forgets to mention that some U.S. Latina/os are Muslims not as the result of conversion, but as the result of being the child of a Muslim parent. While these individuals are not the majority within the present U.S. Latina/o Muslim community, in the next decade or so, non-convert U.S. Latina/o Muslims will be a strong and larger part of this community.

States through the civil rights struggle and its connections with the Nation of Islam. While this connection with the Nation of Islam is less strong now than what it was during the height of the civil rights movement, there are nonetheless some U.S. Latina/o Muslims who come to Islam through the Nation of Islam. At the same time, some argue that, "On an ideological level, [U.S.] Latino Muslims have been profoundly influenced by their African-American counterparts, adopting similar ideas of spiritual self-discovery and emancipation in their approach to Islamic."[3] This contact with African American Muslims during the civil rights era was particularly notable in big cities like New York, where a group of Puerto Rican converts "involved in anti-war protests, civil rights protests, and Puerto Rican nationalist movements" founded la Alianza Islámica, the first grass-roots Latina/o Muslim organization in the United States.[4]

Second, the boom of the Internet in the '90s has connected individuals and communities that likely would not be in contact otherwise. This medium of communication has allowed for U.S. Latina/os to make contact with Muslims groups and have allowed U.S. Latina/o Muslims to actually create their own groups and establish *da'wah* [invitation to Islam through education] to other U.S. Latina/os, especially from younger generations.[5] This fits with anthropologist Karin van Nieuwkerk's argument that, "Many [U.S.] American converts relate that the Internet was a very important medium in their search for information about Islam," and in some cases, "Without the Internet they might not have become acquainted with Islam."[6] The Internet has thus proven to be an important mechanism in the establishment of U.S. Latina/o Muslim communities across the United States, as it has provided a vehicle not only to learn about Islam but also to create a community.[7] Like other Muslim communities

---

3. Aidi, "Olé to Allah," para. 8. The clearest example of this connection is the focus on Africa as the place where their roots lie, even though ancestors of U.S. Latina/o went through Spain before getting to northern Africa. We will analyze this focus on the Moors (Muslims in Spain) in chapter 3.

4. Ibid. I offer a description of this and other organizations in the next chapter.

5. *Da'wah* refers to the dissemination of Islam, which compares to the term proselytizing. But there are differences because, as Yvonne Yazbeck Haddad states, "the goal of da'wa is to win the individual to the truth, not to win the argument." [Haddad, "The Quest for Peace," 22.]

6. van Nieuwkerk, "Gender, Conversion, and Islam," 113.

7. The Internet is so important that even Juan Galván, executive director of the Latino American Da'wah Organization (LADO), wrote an article about the importance of the

in Western societies, U.S. Latina/o Muslims find in the Internet avenues to share their stories, and as "converts can realize themselves not only by testifying to their conversion, but also by finding a place to belong."[8]

Third, because Islam was placed at the forefront of the national narrative after the events of 9/11, many U.S. Latina/os started to look into this religion. Rikani suggests that "most [U.S.] Latinos have come to learn about Islam primarily from their interactions with immigrant Muslims," and that these interactions triggered conversions to Islam.[9] The attitudes towards Muslim immigrants in the United States after 9/11 located them at the margins of society, as "nonpersons." U.S. Latina/os are quite aware of this condition of living as "nonpersons," so U.S. Latina/os who converted to Islam during the months after 9/11, especially in big cities, felt the need to learn about these immigrant communities and their religion in order to understand their marginalization. In other words, a sense of solidarity may have been the trigger for some to start their search into Islam. The last two areas Rikani examines, prison and marriage, "are not restricted to any particular time period."[10] He establishes that most U.S. Latina/o conversions to Islam in prison are related to U.S. African American conversions in prison. This type of conversion, while not the most evident among the U.S. Latina/os during my fieldwork, is important to understand because the conversion to Islam offers prisoners, "an activity structure including such features as prayers and lessons, and an alternative social space within the confinement of the walls."[11] Finally, in the case of conversions through marriage, while Rikani offers different examples of U.S. Latinas who converted due to marriage he finds that such conversions have "not occurred as often as marriage to non-Latino Muslims."[12] These conversions through marriage do not follow a single paradigm as the conversions happen in different ways.

Internet, giving advice about how to use it for *da'wah*. See Galván, "E-Dawah," no pages.

8. van Nieuwkerk, "Gender, Conversion, and Islam," 114.

9. Rikani, "Latino Conversion to Islam," para. 16.

10. Ibid, para. 3.

11. van Nieuwkerk, "Gender and Conversion to Islam in the West," 6.

12. Rikani, "Latino Conversion to Islam," para. 26.

CONVERSION NARRATIVES

Rikani bases his conclusions on his experiences and contact with the U.S. Latina/o Muslim community in Union City, New Jersey, and Puerto Rico, but also the "contact with [U.S.] Latino Muslims in the United States and throughout the world through the medium of the Internet."[13] This is important to acknowledge because the Internet, as mentioned above, was initially the most important vehicle for U.S. Latina/o Muslims to create community, particularly local grassroots organizations. It is through reading blogs and sites dedicated to sharing stories about conversion that many journalists and some scholars, like myself, have attained their initial understandings of the community. The basic aspect of the participation in these cyber-community activities was and in many cases still is the sharing of one's conversion narratives. Through these narratives, U.S. Latina/o Muslims make sense of their conversion and their newfound religion.

The personal character of conversion narratives makes them difficult to understand outside of the individual's story, and I am in no way interested in imposing a particular structure on the narratives that follow. But as Karin van Nieuwkerk states, there are issues that are important to recognize about the construction of conversion narratives:

> First, conversion narratives are created backwards; that is, they are told after the conversion. Past events are reinterpreted in light of current convictions. The stories should therefore not be understood as containing factual information on the conversion process. Second, this reconstructing process does not only take place at the individual level but also at the group level ... Converts come together to discuss their experiences and incorporate common narrative elements into their stories.[14]

These characteristics were evident within the narratives coming out of my fieldwork. The individuals interviewed put together conversion narratives that contextualized their own story in light of their newfound religion. As van Nieuwkerk finds, "Converts do not simply reproduce a rehearsed script but include elements of the new religion's ideological rationale into their narratives."[15] What this means is that individuals will look at their past experiences and attitudes not in light of what was

13. Ibid, para. 3.

14. van Nieuwkerk, "Gender, Conversion, and Islam," 97.

15. van Nieuwkerk, "Gender and Conversion to Islam in the West," 4.

happening in their lives at that time, but through the lenses of the new Islamic perspectives. In the next chapters we will go into detail regarding the process of conversion and the re-construction of identity, but before we begin this analysis it is important to introduce some of these narratives as they help us locate this community and their voices. These narratives bring out into the open the voices of U.S. Latina/o Muslims, which have heretofore been buried and silenced by traditional discourses.[16] We begin with Sonia's story, and then we hear from Roberto, María, Félix, Laura, Pedro, Carol and José. I conclude the chapter with a brief analysis of the power of these conversion narratives as stories and the importance of the narration of these stories in the development and understanding of the U.S. Latina/o Muslim experience.

Sonia

When I came to Islam I was going through a period of searching. I grew up Catholic, devout Catholic, and I was really enthusiastic about that religion. After finishing high school my aspiration was to become a nun, so I decided to go into the convent. Some time later I started feeling different. We prayed almost all day, even though there were some moments to cook and clean. In the times of prayer we had to be in the chapel, and during those times I started feeling like I did not want to be there. I did not want to pray. Everyday I felt the same way but I stayed until they gave us vacation.

Once I got home I told my mom I did not want to go back, that it did not feel right. She was worried and started asking questions: "What happened? Did somebody do something to you?" I answered: "No, everybody treated me great. I just don't feel like I want to pray anymore. I don't want to pray." By that time we got the visa to come to the United States. So, we came to New York. In New York there was not a church group, but I felt like I needed to have God in my life. I felt like I was lost and I needed to search for something. I found a Pentecostal group and I started to meet with them and go to their meetings. It was my first experience with Pentecostals. There were times when the spirit comes to the people and for some reason the lights are off. The person praying for you has his

---

16. These narratives come from my interviews and while I have reconstructed them linguistically, and translated some of them, they represent the actual experience and words of the people, not an analysis of it. In some cases, I have added some context as part of the narratives in order to make sense of the questions I asked.

hand on you and tells you to fall, and you are supposed to fall because of the spirit. When I saw that, I did not fall and I became disenchanted.

I started working in a department store in Manhattan. Most people working at the store were Muslims and since I saw the women with their piece of cloth (*hijab*) I became curious. I asked them: "Where are you from? Where do you come from? Are you from another planet or something like that?" So, they told me that their appearance was in response to Islam and they started giving me pamphlets. I started reading about Islam while at the same time their attitude caught my attention. One time, a client came into the store to return something she bought and she started arguing about the condition of the product. She became aggressive verbally, but my co-worker, a Muslim, stopped her and told her: "One moment, I am a Muslim and Muslims are just, do not lie, and do no harm. If I do you some harm, God is watching me." After listening to this, I was like "Wow, not everyone says this." This attracted me, so I started visiting the mosque, the Islamic Center of New York on 96th Street. They had class for people who wanted to learn about Islam.

One of my preoccupations was that I could not understand the Trinity in Catholicism. I remember asking the priest about it and he would only tell me that I just needed to believe, that religion need not be questioned and that faith need not be questioned. On the contrary, while taking these classes they told me not to believe something just because they tell me to but by investigating and making sure that I find the truth for myself. They told me that when somebody believes is because they are conscious that what it is there is the truth, not because somebody says that it is. Then, I talked to my family and my mom told me: "First, you wanted to be a nun, then Pentecostal, and now Muslim." I told her that this was serious, so she wanted to know what I liked about it. I was clear and told her: "Mom, we have always been Catholics, and we always have in our household some wine or beer or rum that they send from the Dominican Republic. One drinks and nothing happens; one just goes to church to ask for the pardon of the priest. In Islam, if one does something like this, one is sinning. So if one wants to keep the faith like one is supposed to, one has to put aside everything that is prohibited."

I also started talking about pork and that eating it is a sin but if one does not, one is following God's rules. She told me that this makes sense. I also shared the idea about the Trinity because that was the most important thing for me as I was able to start understanding that Jesus is not the

Son of God, but a prophet. This was one of the most difficult things to grasp, and even after taking the *shahadah* (public declaration of faith) it was hard for me to let go of that idea of the divinity of Jesus because all of my life I had been praying to Jesus. I felt bad. I said to myself, "Jesus is going to be mad at me because I am no longer praying to him." But no, in Islam I understood that we are humans and that we only pray to God. In Catholicism, I was really far from what Islam tells us. There was no logic to it. They believe in saints, which one should not believe in or praise. One day in the mosque, once all of those problems and questions were clarified, I decided not to wait anymore because that is what I was looking for. Earlier in my life I used to go to retreats and while at the retreat my faith was really strong but when I left them I felt empty. That always happened. Once I learned about Islam, I studied it and practiced it and to date, twelve years after taking the *shahadah*, I have never felt hollow or empty. Islam filled me. All those [other] things are now in the past and thanks to God I am really happy about accepting Islam.

The same day I took the *shahadah* at the mosque I decided to start wearing the *hijab*. I left the mosque wearing it that hot day and returned home. When my dad saw me, he exclaimed: "Holy! What is wrong with this youngster?" I told him that I had accepted Islam and my mom answered him: "No, leave her alone as that will go away." That was their first impression, but then when my first Ramadan came I felt really good because as I was fasting they were saying: "Sonia is fasting, try not to eat in front of her. Try to respect her." So, with time my family was very happy and respected my decision. Friends and neighbors here in the United States did not have any problems [with what I was doing], but some neighbors back in the Dominican Republic found out and they did respond badly. They challenged my family because we have been Catholics all of our lives and they could not believe why my family would allowed me to leave Catholicism and why they had not "put me in my place." I remember some friends came to visit at our house and when one of them saw me he insulted me. I was so mad that I responded with an insult of my own. Afterwards, I knew that as a Muslim I wasn't supposed to answer back like this but on the contrary I had to forgive. From that moment on, I learned that I had to handle such situations differently. No matter how bad and ugly people's comments are, I have to teach them about the beauty of Islam. Though I have to admit that for the most part, thanks to God, my friends and family have been really respectful towards me. I feel really good about that.

Latina/o y Musulmán

Roberto

My coming to Islam was in 1995. I used to be a driving instructor and it was dangerous. Many of my students were Hindu, and a lot people thought I was going to end up being a Hindu because I was always gathering with Hindus. It was not my interest; it was just that my friends were Hindu. It happened one day that I was teaching a lady from Bangladesh. That was my first physical encounter with a Muslim gathering. It was Ramadan, in April of 1995, because I remember that the celebration for one whole month. I became interested in Islam as I saw a person perform *wudu*, a Muslim's ritual of cleaning before he performs prayers. That is what awakened my interest to this religion. It was also interesting that during prayers, generally speaking, the ladies do not go to the side of the men, and men do not go to the side of the ladies. I have always seen that usually, when men go to the restroom sometimes they use the bathroom and they just come out quick, not even a hand wash. That is disgusting. But, it happens and it is true. On many occasions I was so affected by the way this person was performing his *wudu* and cleaning. I found it so interesting that I asked him to give me some information. He sent me to a *masjid*. There I was given a book, an Islamic book. I read it straight away and it awakened my interest in Islam just by reading it, but I did not make any commitments. I read it for the second time and I felt curiosity that I wanted to be a Muslim, but I still did not make any commitment. It was when I read it for the third time, that I actually felt the need to become a Muslim. So, an interest and curiousity became a need. I embraced Islam in April 1995, and since then, *alhumdulillah* (thanks to God), I am living as a Muslim.

My mom is back in Guatemala but my brothers are here, and after I became Muslim they used to make fun of me. Since our mom taught us to worship one way ever since we were kids, they would ask about the way I worship and even call me *el patito feo* (ugly duckling). I always try to respond to them in the most educated way I can even though they are my family and we get along pretty well. I always tell them: "You know it is not that I am in the black sheep of the family. It is that I have actually come through. You guys, you were taught this, and for you it is a tradition to be what you are. It became a routine in your life since you were kids. That is what we do on Sundays, and that is what we do on these days. So now you guys have to decide whether this is really what you want. That is not your choice. You are just following a tradition. You are what you have been told, what you have been taught." For example, I used to pick up something, anything, and I used to tell them: "Since I was a kid my mom always told me, 'Son, this is black,' and I didn't have a reason not to believe her. She was my mother. I mean how could she be lying to me? But then it came to the point when I went to school and learned the differences in colors and I was able to stand in front of my mom and say, 'Mom, I don't see this as being black anymore. I see it white.' Now, I have my own identity because I learned. When you start applying to yourself what you have learned, that is when you become your real self."

In the end, my brothers did not make much of a problem. My mom, she used to say that it is the religion of the devil. She did not have any clue what she was saying. She used to say that we were Satan and whatever. I said: "Mom, I am going to tell you back what you used to tell me. You always told me never to judge anything before you know what you are talking about. Why are you saying this is the religion of Satan when you have no clue what Islam is? Can you tell me what Islam is?" "Well, it's what you are in." She replied. So, I decided to ask her: "I know it is what I am in. But can you tell me what it is?" She realized her mistake and she realized that I had changed.

I was not a heavy drinker but I used to drink occasionally. I smoked all the time, everywhere. As I came and found myself more as a Muslim, I learned that my body is given to me as *amana* (contract for the transfer of property). It is entrusted to me. On the Day of Judgment I have to answer for what I did with what was entrusted to me. So, if I kept smoking and put cancer into this body, something that was given to me as a trust, and I give it back old and rotten, I am going to have to pay for that. I do not want to be liable for something that I can take care of during my stay here in this world. I learned that the more you do to endanger yourself, like when you drink and you get behind the wheel, you are endangering yourself and you are endangering others more. If you kill yourself, you are going to have to answer for that. It came to the point that I decided to change my name to a Muslim's name. That was *la gota que colmó la copa* for members of my family.

I did not understood what was the big deal. My uncles and aunts came after me: "Do you know how long your mother was thinking about your name when she was carrying you for nine months? Do you know the whole list of names she went through?" I reacted: "I mean, what is a name? Am I any different? Do I love you guys any less because I am no longer what I was and I am Roberto? Does it make any difference?" They said: "Well, no." "Then," I responded, "what's the point?" Everybody was always saying that I betrayed the family. The betraying the family accusation really hit me hard because I love my family. I love my family a lot. My uncles, my nieces, my cousins, my aunts, and every member of my family that came from the family tree, I love them all. I love my family. For most of them to come out and say that I was betraying the family, crushed me. So I started segregating myself from my family. Nowadays, *alhumdulillah*, it is amazing. You know how my younger brother used to make fun of me because I changed my name? [Well, I reminded him that] Mohamed Ali changed his name from Cassius Clay to Mohamed Ali. Now, my younger brother asks me questions: "What does Islam say about this? When a Muslim is fasting, what do you do in this case?" It makes me realize that my embracing Islam has also affected my family. They ask questions that they did not have in their minds before. I have prayed that sooner or later either one of my brothers, my nieces, or my cousins will want to follow my steps and take the *shahadah*, *Insha'Allah* (God willing). I have been an example to them. Whatever I am doing, I explain them why I am doing it. I have become an example for many members of my family and that is why I hope that, *Insha'Allah*, one of them will follow in my steps.

Up to now, there are no problems. I just wish I could travel back home. I bought my mother a Qur'an. She asked me: "Ok, do you guys believe in Jesus?" She asked because that is the first thing that people put between Islam and Christians, do you believe in Jesus? I answered: "Yes, mother and guess what? We also believe that he is coming back for a second time." She was excited: "Do you really?" It mad such a big impact on her that now she asks me more questions. I spent a pretty good time [with her], but it was just roughly two weeks. She was very impressed with the knowledge that Islam has, comparing it to what Christianity has. Now, she realizes that Islam is not the religion of Satan.

Regarding the question of being a Latino and a Muslim, I am clear about it. What is a Latino? It is just a name given to you because of the language you were born into. So, if you just happen to be a Latino born in Europe, does that make you less Latino? If you are a Latino born in the U.S., does that make you less Latino? No. Latino in reality has to do with the language, basically. It is just like the Prophet Mohamed said about being an Arab. Who is an Arab? An Arab is anyone who speaks Arabic.

So, you do not necessarily have to be born in Saudi Arabia or to any of the Arabic countries in order to be an Arab, according to Prophet Mohamed's statement. If you learn Arabic you are an Arab. The same applies to Latino. A Latino, or a wannabe Latino, is anyone who speaks Spanish. I consider myself a Muslim first. Latino comes second. How do I identify myself as a Latino? Just by hearing me talking you know I am a Latino. When we have events where the Latino people get together, like a fundraising dinner for example, how do you know it is a Latino gathering? If you see a lot of people eating Pollo Loco, you know you are at a Latino fundraising event. The food that you eat, the togetherness of people when they are having a meeting, that is what it means to be a Latino. Speaking the Latin language or the Spanish language, that constitutes being a Latino. A Muslim is anyone who believes in the religion of Islam and submits to it, just as God gave it to us. If you believe and apply it to your life, you are a Muslim. Therefore, you are Muslim first, Latino second.

It is important, very important, that we, as Muslims with a Latino background, understand that we have an advantage. Remember the Gold Rush in California? Those days, I mean there was so much gold over here. Imagine all the gold that was around California and very few gold diggers. But, as soon as a few gold diggers came in, they found there was enough gold. They went back to their lands. They spread the word and more started to come in, until they actually ran out [of gold]. Why am I relating being a Muslim to the Gold Rush? Because Islam is like a gold rush and we are the gold diggers. The gold is our countries that do not know anything about Islam. We have the advantage of being able to go back to our countries, tell people about it and spread Islam in a way that nobody ever thought about. Islam is the fastest growing religion according to some surveys. So, to me, the people are the gold. We are the gold diggers. We have so much to work with.

María

I reverted to Islam about five or six years ago, here in New York. I was single at the time and I met a Muslim brother who became my friend. I had not really come across any Muslims. Well, I'm sure that I had but not anyone that had some identifying characteristic as a Muslim, like wearing a *hijab* (head covering). This Muslim brother and I began to talk, and once in a while we would touch upon the religion. I would ask him questions about some definitions and practices. He would give me short answers, but the answers he would give me affected me because he was very, very, very sincere. It was a sincerity I had never seen in anyone, and my family is a pretty religious family. He would not go into detail too much about Islam because he said: "I don't want to influence you. Everybody comes to Islam his or her own way in life. However, why don't you read?" So, I started reading about it and going online, and started talking to other Muslims. I started being pulled in. I was sort of being sucked in. As I came across Latino Muslims, I started realizing that this was not something that was an Arab religion, which is the perception one takes from the media and everyone else.

I just continued to research and study. I looked at it from different perspectives. As a woman, I need to know how things are going to fill me, and my needs of a woman. As a Latina, a Puerto Rican, I feel we have special needs that other nationalities do not. So, I started researching and everything started to make sense to me. Now, I am a pretty analytical person so it is not like I heard the verses of the Qur'an and all of a sudden I started to convert. I mean that happens to a lot of people and that is beautiful, but that did not happen to me. I was continuously researching, but it was a research that I could not put away. Even at times, I would put the materials away, and I would say: "Forget this, I have other things to do." Within a couple of days it was like I had to go back to it, a project I had to continue to finish it. Then, I started coming across more Latino Muslims especially in New Jersey. So, aside of just making sense to me, it became very practical. It was a way of life that reminded me very much of the way my family was when I was growing up. Our morals were very high. Things like dating, premarital sex, and children out of wedlock do not exist in my family. Even my uncles do not believe men and women should be friends because they are just that strict. We grew up Catholic, but some of my family members are Pentecostal.

It reminded me very much of my family's morality and the way I was growing up. After that it was a slow progression. After about a year and a half, aside from it making sense to me, it was something that took my heart completely. I was completely afraid. I was going against what people perceived to go hand in hand, Puerto Rican and Christian. I did not know how my family was going to react but it was something I couldn't not do. I do not think I had ever felt that way about anything before. I converted, but it was not until a year and half later that I began to take my new faith seriously. By seriously, I mean in terms of saying my prayers on time. The *hijab* I did not wear until 2004 after returning from *hajj* in Saudi Arabia.

How did my family respond? My family is a very well rounded family. Of course I had family members who politely told me: "You know this goes against our religion, our beliefs that Jesus is the Son of God." But, it was never anything like "Oh, you are *basura* (trash)." My family has never been that way, and I cannot say that I have had a bad experience like other people have had bad experiences. I do not think that is always the case, especially for Latinos here. But I have come across a lot of my friends in Puerto Rico who had that same experience. They have converted and it was not a big issue to the family members. Other people have had bad experiences. My family did not try to talk me out of it, but they expressed concern in a very polite manner. Once I started to become serious and progress [in my newfound faith] they realized nothing about me that was good changed, and I was still actively participating in my family's life. Even with issues like the eating habits I have had no problems. My family is not big on pork, so it is not a big thing for them. It has been like five or six years and my family will make a pot of rice that has no pork for me or they will make it all with no pork at all. They will cook just anything like that. And, if something has pork and I do not know about it, they will run to me and be like: "No, no, no don't touch that, it has pork." They know how serious I am about this.

Christianity dominates my family in terms that if something bad happens in the world, they turn to the words in the Bible. I do not refute anything. I just simply nod my head and I understand that they are coming from their perspective. At the same time, when I speak I always say what the Qur'an says about the issue so that they know. Not that it is a competition, but I seek for them to know my life, my present background, where I stand.

Regarding my friends' reaction to my conversion, I have to say that I have not encountered any major issues. Only one asked me: "Why are you wearing that thing on your head?" I think that was simply out of fear, fear that now our relationship has changed. But, a friend of mine the other day told me: "You know, we're now different. We have different viewpoints in terms of religion, but we're still the same in terms of our friendship." I do not think I really changed that much. I still hang out with my friends but we were never the type to be in clubs. So, that has not been like cold water in their faces since that has never been my style anyway. It has not been too much of a difference except now I do not celebrate Christmas. I do not go to church and things like that. Just that may be the biggest difference.

Regarding how reversion affected my Latino identity, I have to say that I do not feel it has been affected. Actually, I feel it has reinforced my identity because in my perspective I am actually going back to my roots. I think people who are Christian, who are Catholic, have gone away from their Latino roots because we have our roots in Spain. We have our roots in the Moors. Our language contains Arabic words. Our morality, our chivalry, the men, their protection, how they are with their women, with their families, that comes from the Arabs, from the Moors. So, I think I have reinforced my existing identity. I think I am in an uphill battle because some people's perspectives are now the norm and that is what I am dealing with. But, I do not feel displaced or like I am going against my Latino roots. My identity is clear: I am Muslim first, and I am Puerto Rican second.

As a woman I am also conscious that there is the perception that Muslim women are oppressed, but I do not see it that way. Christianity says the downfall of humanity is due to the woman. That is a hard load to carry for the rest of your life as a woman. Islam says that it was not the fault of Eve; it was Adam and Eve that succumbed to the devil's temptation. Let's say that it was Eve who offered the apple to Adam; the fact that he took it is his own responsibility. That fact that she took hers is her own responsibility. Everyone is responsible for their own actions and responsible for their own sin, and it is interesting that in Islam, people are responsible for their worship and their prayers. Men and women are equally responsible. In Christianity, a woman is responsible for everything and yet she can also be told what to do since she is seen as being beneath a man. Islam is different in that way. Christianity is so engraved in our minds that one does not seem to question that sort of injustice.

In terms of the *hijab*, it is not oppressive; in fact, wearing it forces people to deal with you in response to what you say and what you do. No one can see what your hair looks like or what your beauty looks like, which is what sometimes guides people's judgments. Women have to wear *hijab* because God commands it. No man can force you to wear *hijab*. If there are men who force you to wear *hijab*, it does not count. That is why men cannot force women. They know that in the Qur'an, in the eyes of God, it does not count. It is a woman's choice. So, if a man is forcing her there is really no reason because it earns her no points. If the woman is not doing it for the sake of Allah, then it does not work. But, you see women walking around wearing *hijab* and wearing *niqab*, and many are not married. So, who is forcing them to wear these things? No one is forcing them. It is their relationship with God.

The community is growing here in the city. I know is different from other places; it is a different type of animal, a different mentality. We are faster here. We are always just in a rush and things like that. So, I think in the city area is only natural that one can convert because you come across other people. It is just much more natural. I do think the Latino population and the Latino Muslims are spreading to more areas because they move for work, or for whatever other reasons. It is not just a trend because the attention that the community is getting seems to indicate that it is going to continuously grow.

A lot of people think that, especially for women: "*Oh, se casó con un arabe y por eso* [she married an Arab and that is why], she is Muslim." That is of course the case for some, even for some men too, but that is not true of the majority of cases. In the majority of cases people say that they have found not only a way of life, but that it is a way of life that makes sense and that they know. Except for wearing *hijab* or whatever, things that involve a Muslim and his life are not different from things that involve Latinos. This is why Latinos can marry Arabs. They will point out, specifically people from the Caribbean like *puertorriqueños*: "Man, you know, you are just like us." We have the same mentality, especially with the Arabs from Africa. And I tend to assume that's simply because we have African obviously in us. I met a group of Moroccans and they were like so many Puerto Ricans. I told them: "You guys are just like us, there are hardly any differences [between us] except the language, whatever, and maybe the religion." But in terms of the men, the way they protect and lead the family, and the women, *sencilla, humilde,* you know, caring, take care of the family--those roles are very much a part of a Muslim's life. And so you will find a bunch of Latinos who come to Islam because it's like a transition. It wasn't a big transition for me to become a Muslim; it was a life I was leading already because I am a *Boricua* and my family is this way. I have told my family, especially one uncle of mine: "Dude, you are a Muslim, you just do not even know it. This is exactly how a Muslim acts." They laugh; they laugh because they find it funny.

29

Félix

I became Muslim right after high school. I was nineteen years old at the time. My family is actually around ninety percent Protestant, really strong Protestants. So I grew up as a Protestant and I studied with the Protestants. In high school, I got exposed to Islam through a Bolivian friend. He actually entered the Nation of Islam. The guy was white so I don't know how he entered the Nation of Islam. It was through him that I learned about Islam and he was very influential in my life. After learning about it, I studied Islam and after two years I became Muslim.

Once I told my family about my conversion, it was not a big shock because I had been preparing them for a while. I would say, "Do you know that Muslims believe in Moses and Jesus, too?" My dad was like yeah, yeah. So, I kind of prepared them because I knew something was going to happen. When I converted, I told my sister, and my sister went to my dad and told him, "Do you know that Felix became a Muslim?" He called me and since he was watching his *tele-novela* he asked me to tape it before turning the TV off. He told me, "So, I hear you became one of those guys that worship cows and all of those stuff, right?" I was like, "Those are Hindus. The Hindus, they do that." And so all that my dad said was, "As long as you don't worship the devil or Satan, I'm happy with that." He actually did not believe that I was going to change. But, within two weeks, he came back to me and said, "You know this is the first week in five years that I have slept real nice." He actually used to wait for me, coming back from clubs at five in the morning. When he heard me turn off the car once I got home, I could see the light turn off in his room and only then would he go to sleep. One time, my brother-in-law told my mom that he thought that I had left Islam, so she ran to me and said, "You better not leave Islam." So, I was really happy that actually the whole family kind of accepted it, at least my immediate family, but not the other ones. From the others came all the jokes. Oilman, camel and Pakistani; I heard it all. They refer to me as "this oilman." My friends, many of them, converted to Islam, so there were no problems with them. They would ask many questions, and I liked that very much because it was because of these conversations that they converted.

Regarding my identity, I think that Islam has actually enhanced the way I look at my roots. By that I mean that like the prophet Mohamed, peace be upon him, he came to perfect good character. Islam is here to perfect you as an individual no matter of what nationality you are. As a Latino, Mexican, Chicano, or whatever, you leave all the bad stuff, the stuff that has killed our people throughout the ages. You leave the alcohol and all the other bad stuff. When I became Muslim, I still did wrong everyday, but at least I became conscious that I am not supposed to do the bad stuff, or the little stuff continuously. So, I try to stay away from those things. In a sense, like everyone else here is saying, I now have the moral responsibility to find out about my roots, my history, all of my sides.

My uncles and my grandfathers were alcoholics. They were Christian; they were Catholic. Was there anything stopping them from doing that? People won't find a prohibition in the teachings of Christianity, but in Islam there is one. Do not drink! It is forbidden point blank. So, it is a clear channel and again, it does not force me but it almost guides me to do the research about my people, my family, and my history. It makes it better for my kids and my kids' kids. It makes the path very clear. Do not go there because obviously there are a lot of thorns. Do not go there because there is a cliff. Stay on the path. Islam has ennobled me because I no longer pray to the porcelain god on weekends like I used to. It brings me up a notch as far as the human chain. I just think that definitely Islam has ennobled me as regards who I am as a Latino. Now, I have that responsibility to teach Latinoness, or Chicanoness or the whateverness to my kids because they are part of it and they need to be proud. We need to be able to speak Spanish, Japanese, or whatever other language that we happen to know and pass it on because now it is part of the responsibility that rests on our shoulders. We have to keep it up. It is a lot of work. Everyday we have to be on our toes but it is something worth fighting for.

Like people have been saying, Islam opens our minds. Through ourselves we are finding out who we really are. It is almost like a rebirth of our culture. We are going back to the more traditional fundamentals where we are coming from. In a sense, culture and religion are two different things. People do not ask me: "What is your religion or what is your culture?" Now, if I say my last name, they won't ask me: "Are you Christian or are you Muslim?" They automatically know I am a Latino. But, if I tell them that I am a Muslim, then they start questioning: "Well, you have a Spanish name, so what are you?" So, you see what I am saying? To them, because of my Spanish name, it does not matter what religion I am. I will always be a Latino. Now, I think for us Islam is what actually brings it together. It is like cleaning, where the good things are kept and the bad things are put aside. It is the same way for Christians, Protestants, because they do not remain the same. They change a lot of stuff. They do not do this; they do not do that. And, that is the same thing with us. We do not do a lot of things. But, being Latino is not something you change.

I do not see it on the basis of whether one is Muslim first or a Latino first, because one is born into it. See what I am saying? I do not have a choice. I have a choice to pick religion or not, but I do not have the choice to be a non-Latino. I do not know how that would translate. So, what I am trying to say is that it is not like you are a Latino or a Muslim. Those are two separate things. But, when it comes, it makes your mind clearer. Now, I am a Latino and I should be proud of my roots. I want to learn more. I do not think there are other religions that actually do that.

Laura

I was waiting for something I could not find. I was disappointed at something. I was in church because it was a thing of my parents. Both of my parents were very religious as they were pastors in Peru. I have always seen them at the head of the church and for a while I was very happy to be with them in Peru. It was a Pentecostal church and within it the people share their needs. Things changed when I came to the United States. Here, people are a little bit different. There were cultural issues and words I did not understand in my own Spanish. In time I adapted and I attended a Presbyterian church, but comparing this church with the one in Peru, I felt like it did not fulfill me spiritually. I mean, I had to follow a ritual from the church and everything was more material. On Sundays I spent time worrying about what I was going to wear and when I was in church it was not like in Peru where in the Pentecostal church I was clapping. In this church I did not clap. But, again I adapted to the rhythm of the service and I becamed used to it.

While in Peru I had been a Sunday school teacher and a leader of the youth group, so I had to change and adapt to a new church where nobody knew me. The one thing I continued doing was singing. I was soloist, so I kept singing with my guitar as I received invitations to do so in different places. But, even in the midst of this I was still empty because I felt that everything here was more superficial, more into the material stuff. Another thing that did not fulfill me was that when my dad studied in the seminary he told me about the history of the church. That is when

I learned about the Holy Trinity, and things that were not in congruence with my beliefs while I was a child. Being a younger adult and learning about all these things that I did not know, like how the Holy Trinity was formed and modified by religious people, and about the existence of myths within the Bible. All of a sudden I was questioning what was real and true. Now, I was disappointed, so I was going to church to socialize or for my presentations. But, at this time, I did not even believe in the things I sang about because I sang about Jesus and all of that stuff. I started to be away from the church, even if my dad stayed within the church because he liked the ministry and the work in the community.

I stopped going to church and became, as many people say, more materialistic. As I became disappointed by my faith, that which I had had from my childhood, and as I learned that most of those things I believed in do not exist, I felt empty. It was a phase of about a year until I heard about Islam and it was through my husband. Now, even before learning about Islam I had believed Jesus was a messenger, a prophet. Before, I believed that Jesus was the father and that the father was the one that heard my prayers and that is why I had all the blessings and miracles. "But how do I pray now?" Before Islam, I prayed: "God, forgive me because I do not know how to pray. I do not know if when I pray is in the name of the father or the son because I do not believe. But, forgive me, if I do right or wrong. I believe that something gives me life; I believe someone gave me existence."

But when I heard about Islam, about Islam being mission to God, I said: "Exactly right." We exist under the will of a supreme being, and that made sense to me. I asked my husband: "Do you believe in heaven?" Because I was so materialistic I did not get it. It was then that I found answers in Islam to many of the questions I had. In Islam, as a woman one is more modest, and the picture I have of myself before is totally different. Before Islam, I was worried about the kind of clothes I was going to buy because I worked at an American company of accessories and fashion. I was attentive to my nails, my hair, and the clothes I was going to wear, focusing on the name of the brand, like Christian Dior. Those dresses can cost over $200. But, that was not my focus in Islam.

The first time I went to a congregation to pray, to pray to God, I saw the women praying, and that picture impressed me. I remember that first time because I knew I had come to this place to worship God. Even today I get emotional remembering seeing those women praying.

It doesn't matter; you enter without shoes. Before, I was worried about what shoes I was going to wear to church because all of the women were in fashion. That was my concern then, but here it was all about the spiritual. That is what caught my attention about these women praying. Leaving that place I did my first *jumah*. That day I did not care if people saw me crying because people were so concentrated on their prayers. I do not think people saw me crying but I left that place crying. I cried, and it was the prayer of *Athan* that touched me. I thought: "What is this? What is this? I cannot understand the language, but this is something, this is definitively for me. I had studied it but I had been missing the congregation, being there in the house of God. I am not worried about my hair anymore. I am covered, with simple clothes. This is what caught my attention, the spiritual part. That was what fulfilled me, so I said: "This is mine." That is how I found Islam.

In my case, I had no problems with my family because they are in Peru. I told my dad that I was going to the mosque and doing my prayers in the mosque. My dad told me that it was ok and that there were different religions to get to God and only one God. He started to read the Qur'an because he likes to read and observe new things. He said: "Wow, how interesting that the Qur'an starts, In the name of God, the most merciful." He got really interested in what he was reading and one time he came to visit me at my house, and he saw my husband praying when the time for prayers came. He said: "What a good discipline your husband has for prayer. What a good discipline." So, there were no problems on my dad's side. My mom who was in Peru, I did not tell her that I was a Muslim because there the words Islam and Muslim are associated with terrorism. So, I told her that I was going to the temple with my husband to worship to God, and there I do my prayers. But, about a year ago I told her: "Mom, I am a Muslim and I cover myself. One day we are going to see each other and I cover myself." My mom told me: "Wow, you still believe in Jesus? Yes mom, I still believe in Jesus. He is a great messenger, a prophet. But my prayer is directly to God."

So, my mom already knows. I told my brother at the same time I told my dad. My friends, especially the ones I made in school after coming to this country, thought that I had converted to Islam because of my husband. They did not understand that it was a decision based on my own conviction. That was their idea and I could feel they looking at me with suspicious eyes: "Laura, if you have converted to Islam, we respect you for that." But I distanced myself from them because we did not share a lot of things in common. For example, if we had some social gatherings there were some clashes. One of my friends would ask about my husband not drinking because among Latinos it is a cultural custom for men to have a drink when they gather. Because of that she considered the gathering boring and she actually distanced herself from me.

I had my friends from school. At the time I was a Muslim but I did not cover myself. I mean I covered myself to go to the mosque and I dressed more conservatively in general. It was not that from one day to another I covered myself and put on long clothes. I dressed more conservatively but I felt uncomfortable because in our small groups we were at restaurants and there were drinks. These were my friends, both men and women, from college. For example, after graduation we would meet to celebrate promotions or something like that and they would ask me: "You are just drinking water?" These exchanges made me really uncomfortable because our conversations became more and more characterized by silence as we did not share a lot of things. I decided to distance myself from these friends. Even when they asked about me, I would find some excuse because I felt really uncomfortable. So, I disappeared because even if I was in the same places with them I did not do the same things as them or share anything with them. After this, I started to put all of my interest in my Muslim friends. I do still share a friendship with a Christian friend that works in her church and I remember that it was her mother, who is also a pastor's wife, who told me that I should go to the same place of worship as my husband. She is the only one I have kept in contact with, who knows about me. She asks me: "Are you still a Muslim?" I answer: "Yes." She says that I should not be worried because she is ecumenical.

Pedro

I came into Islam gradually. I was born Catholic and then I followed a Native American way of life. I was a shaman for about five to six years, which is a parallel to Islam. What convinced me that it was easy to jump the fence was that the Native American people, their message and all these good role model traits were handed down from generation to generation by voice. There was no written scripture. I started to hang out with this guy. He went through different changes. He was Buddhist for a while; he was this, and he was that. He finally settled in Islam and when I met him he started to explain to me how the Qur'an went about it. The message was written 1,400 years ago without changing. When it was written, it was revised by the Prophet, reviewed by the Prophet during twenty-three years of his life, and revealed through the angel Gabriel. The Prophet reviewed none of the other books at the time of the revelation. So, that is how I came to Islam. I have now been a Muslim for about twelve years.

My coming to Islam has been good for our family. Obviously, we are born into the religion of our parents. I went to a Catholic school, being raised in Guadalajara and did the whole church thing. We had the youth group, the Sunday masses, with the guitars and the whole nine yards growing up. When I came to Islam it was in Oregon. I was living away from my family. It was about six months after I took shahadah that I started kind of telling my mom about it. She would always ask me: "Oh, have you gone to church?" I would always argue that God is everywhere and you can pray anywhere as long as the place is clean. But, with time I was boiling up to the point that I finally told her that I became a Muslim. There was an impact, obviously with a lot of questions: "Why did you do that? What? You didn't get it going to Catholic school? Didn't we teach you? You know you had an uncle who was a bishop." I said: "Mom, it does not make me any different. There is only one God. You pray directly to him." These were the things I said over the phone before we finally hung up. They kind of accepted it up to a point.

When I first came down here as a Muslim they were watching me, seeing what I was going to do. They would see me walk to the back room to do my prayers. Now, when the stuff really hit the fan was when some brothers invited me to a *jumah* for a few days. We ended in Lancaster. They gave me a brown robe that was almost the same color as the Franciscan, which is brownish, but it was a little bit different. I thought that it was cool. So, I get home and I have this thing on. I am walking and my dad is sitting there and my mom is there, and they are like, "Oh my God!" They gave me this look from head to toe. I said: "Hi Mom, hi Dad." At that time, I hooked up with the other organization. I had literature, and I am bringing boxes back and forth. But, this thing, coming in with this, dressed up as I was, it was the limit. They just could not wait to get me at the right time: "What the hell are you thinking?" Obviously, [that conversation] did not go too well.

About three days later, I was like: "Here I am." They started: "What is wrong with you? "Don't you see people, our neighbors and everybody, are watching? . . . The people outside, those people are looking. There are some people who are not as understanding as we are." I responded: "Mom, I have been here now for a couple of months. Have you seen any change in me?" She answered: "Yeah!" "So, have you seen change that is bad?" I replied. She went on to say: "No. On the contrary, you are still you but there is more respect, and you are more tolerant." I kept going: "Well, if that brown thing had come with a little rosary on it as a belt and the little white thing, would you have had a problem with it?" She immediately said: "Well, no. Why would I? Francisco is a missionary." I said: "Okay. Well, just pretend I am a missionary because our responsibility as a Muslim is to enlighten people by education about the religion, by way of peace." The friction died down a little bit and then some months later I invited them to come to a presentation as an introduction to Islam. Things really started to relax a little bit, including my father. He would never ask me the questions directly. He would ask my mom to ask me, and went about in that way. I do not know if he does that on purpose or not.

The family was really respectful. For example, when they order pizza, they would take off the pepperoni. Some members of the family even stopped going to the birthdays and their social gatherings even if in my family it is a thing of tradition to participate in these activities, like if they do not get drunk, they are not happy, they are not having fun. Most of the food they eat is either made with or friend in lard, like *chicharrones*, y *patitas de puerco*. Since we cannot eat that, they just stopped preparing it because they wanted to avoid confrontation with me when I came over. Otherwise they would ask, "Oh, aren't you going to eat?" And I would say: "Oh, well we kind of had a salad and we ate before we came over." Or another time they would say, "Here, have a beer. What is wrong with one beer? Oh, your religion? Oh, come on, it is just natural." So, it sometimes became rather a debate, a challenge. It was better to avoid it.

We are five, three sisters and a brother. One of the sisters told me: "I don't care about your religion, but you were born this way and this is what we are. The thing is that I don't want to hear about your religion and I don't want you to tell my kids." She has two kids. This reminds me of another one of my sisters. Her kids see us praying and they go un-wrap a little carpet and want to do what we are doing. One time my mom says: "Come on kids. Come on kids. Let's go. They're going to do their thing. Let's go. Let's leave them alone." I told her: "Mom, why don't you let them see something, even if it's something new? Maybe they'll learn something. They'll learn something good. Is this something bad that they might learn?" So, she relaxed some. Both of my parents are old. They are eighty something years old. Purposely, I would read literature and Qur'an, and leave stuff on the table, not to force matters but like a cake: if it is there maybe they will eat it, maybe not. And, one day she said: "Well, why do I have to change my religion? I am reading your book and the Bible, and they are all very much similar." You can always expand on what you already know, not just go by what you were told growing up. There is still a bit of opposition in my family, mainly from my brother and sisters. My mom and dad, they are cool with it.

Some issues have come from my family back in Mexico. About five years ago, I had the chance to go to Mexico. I had not been in Guadalajara for about, I do not know, fourteen years. I visited some of the relatives, but I mainly stayed home and spent time going out with my cousin who is a lot, like fifteen years, older than I am. He was very outspoken and kept making reference to my religion: "Oh, look at the Taliban. I am going to introduce you to my cousin the Taliban. You know, my cousin is Taliban, so don't say anything because he's got connections and all the bombs. Hey, you want to get wiped out, keep on talking that way about me because my cousin is here." I mean, the whole time he was like that.

The truth is that that conversion has really changed my life and I have fine-tuned some of the actions. Obviously, the diet has been refined, but it has not made me any less Mexican or any less Latino. I was born in Chicago, and raised in Guadalajara. I was raised in the Mexican community and then came back here and I have been hanging around Latinos. Has Islam changed me? I have not gone out to try to be an Arab or try to be a Pakistani. I get gifts, like that dress thing and I hear sometimes: "Oh, don't wear that because it doesn't seem Latino." Hey, it is like if someone gives me a sweater I will wear it once in a while. I am not going to wear it all the time. As far as change, I do not think I have changed the way I am as regards Mexican practices. Well, the change, like I said before, came in my diet, so I do not eat *frijoles con manteca*. Actually, my sister still does eat that so I do not have breakfast at her house. It is like they already know, so they do not push the issue.

[Responding to another interviewee's assessment about the role of TV in the attitude of her parents:] That is the whole idea. Maybe your parents or my parents, they usually stay on the Spanish channels, and these channels whatever they say about Islam or Muslims is not good. They are always: "Look at those Muslims. See? They are always killing; they shoot. Oh, look what they did." But, they do not show on TV that every Ramadan all the Islamic centers go downtown to take care of four, five thousand people. They give them clothes; they give them food. During Katrina, or any other hurricanes, they were all getting together every month to help.

Carol

I have been a Muslim for almost two years actually. When I was in New York, I was working in a country club as a waitress. There were these two co-workers, and I heard people saying that they were Taliban. I had heard about that but I did not really care or pay attention to what it was. So, one day, after the main course we started talking, and suddenly we started talking about religion. They started talking about Jesus. I got my answer about Jesus because I was always confused about the idea of Jesus being three, being God Himself, and the son and all that stuff. It did not really click; I did not believe it made sense to me as a Catholic. After that, I got interested in Islam. I went to a bookstore, and I got some books. I read the Bible, and I started reading the Qur'an. After that, I decided to convert.

When I converted I had been here for just a short period of time. I did not know how to pray then. Later on, I went back to New York and I learned more. I started to pray using just a bandana on my head. Although it was summer, I got used to wear long sleeved shirts and pants, so dressing was not a problem. The problem started when I came back home and I did not take off the bandana. Since my brother-in-law also lives in the house, I could not take off the bandana unless I was in my room, or he was away working. At that time, my sister asked: "Why are you wearing that thing on your head the whole time?" I simply answered: "Because I changed my religion." I started explaining a little bit to her but she just replied: "I accept your religion and whatever you believe in is ok, but just take off that thing on your head. It makes you look ugly." My mother was also not happy about me covering. She would actually tell my little niece: "Go, tell your aunt to take that thing off her head." One day, I had had it. It was the evening and we were supposed to go out as a family. My sister, she just talked so much that day that I just decided to take it off to go with them. But the truth is that I could not take it. I could not take it. I felt like I was just wearing a bikini. It was really bad. It was really bad. When we came back I put it on and since then I have not taken it off. I continue to make more effort to put the whole headscarf.

I went back to New York and then came back to Los Angeles. When I came back, I was wearing the whole thing. My brother went to pick me up at the airport and he did not say anything. He is just one of those guys that believes that if you do not mess with him, he will not mess with you, so you do with your life whatever you want. He did not say anything. When my mother saw me come in the house, she looked at me, I gave her a hug and she just could not say anything. She could not say anything. But, with my mother, it was with her I had the most problems. For example, one day I was going to work and I just took a shower. As I was getting ready to put on the headscarf she said: "I don't know why you wear that thing on your head. You look so beautiful without it." I tried to explain it a little bit: "You know how when grandma used to go to the church, she used to wear a veil on her head." She rapidly responded: "But, think about it. She only did it when she went to church, not the whole day." I retorted: "Well, it is a little bit different, Mom, because the religion that I have mandates that we should cover our heads and our body." She interrupted me: "But, not everybody follows that religion, so why do you do it?" I even told her that they were not supposed to be eating pork either. To this she responded: "I don't know who invented it, but I got the idea to eat the pork, so we eat it." I tried not to be so aggressive with her. She is my mother. I try to be easy on her and just listen to her, so now I tend to respond with: "Yes, mom. Yes, mom." She used to say that she was worried because of the people I was hanging out with. I asked her: "Mother, what do you see? I don't go out at night. I don't drink. I don't smoke. You don't see me going out with guys. What are you worried about?" So, she would point out that she was worried because of the things that people say on TV. I told her: "Well, don't worry about it. I'm here. Look what am I doing. If I'm doing something wrong, then tell me."

My father, he blames a lot of things on my headscarf. My sister she just does not really care. She does not bother, just like my brother. The father of my kids was a different story. He also did not want the headscarf. That is the thing that bothers him the most. Other than that, *alhumdu-lillah*, the kids are being raised on the straight path. I do not have any complaints from him about the kids or how they behave. Basically I have no major issues with my family, but I get worried when other people start saying stuff and they tell my mother. That is the worst because if they say it to me, it would be different, but not to my mother because it makes my mother feel bad. That is what I do not like.

Regarding my identity, I have to say that for me it does not really matter where one is born. What matters is what you are. When I was in New York, I did not have that many Hispanic or Latino friends. I like people for who they are and how they behave. Anyways, I see myself as a Muslim first. I mean I do feel Mexican when I hear the national anthem, but I am Muslim, just like that.

José

I converted to Islam on April 22, 1994, from a Catholic background. Ever since I was a kid, Catholicism did not make much sense to me. I was still looking for a way of life that was going to make sense to me. I started looking into Catholicism around that time, at the end of 1993. Again, I needed guidance but became disillusioned and around the same time I started learning about Islam. Within about three months, I became Muslim after just learning and reading about it, talking to other friends who were Christian, Jehovah's Witnesses, and Muslims. So, in this sense, it was a pretty short trip to Islam.

Now, before I became a Muslim, I was fasting and, as I said, I was reading about Islam. I was living with one of my aunts. After I became a Muslim, one of my sisters told me that this aunt I was living with had called my mom and told her that I was doing drugs, becoming a terrorist, and growing a beard. I found out about how my mom felt afterwards. My brothers and sisters have always been very supportive. No matter what we do we support each other, and that is beautiful. My uncle and aunt that I was staying with became stronger Catholics because they saw my conversion to Islam as a questioning of their beliefs. And so, they became really really Catholic, which I see as a good thing. My mom was very sad because she felt that because I was not a Catholic, I was not going to go to heaven. But she saw the changes. When I would go to visit, in the past, before I was Muslim, I would go and stay maybe a couple hours and then I would go down to the strip bar or go party with friends. I was not even at the house. After I became a Muslim, I would spend all my time with her and she appreciated it. There are a lot of addictions, a lot of *cosas malas*, in the *familia*. But *alhumdulillah*, I was very blessed to become a Muslim because if not I would be out there, probably not even in this country.

My friends were very supportive after I became Muslim. Even as I was getting into my Chicano roots, it has been really good. A few of them, especially my family in Mexico, are still kind of ignorant about Islam, with the "terrorist" frame of mind. There is a lot of ignorance about Islam, but all in all, it has been good all the way around.

I think one of the mistakes people make is to argue that when one is a Muslim, one is not a Latino anymore. One is born a Latino, so it is like your skin color; you do not choose what color you are. That is what you are put into, like you are put into a particular nationality. It is not a choice. It is not as if you are more or less Latino. It is just that you are a Latino. Being a Muslim is a choice. I think religion is one thing and your identity is another. I do not think Islam makes me feel less Latino. It does empower who you are. Now, I know who I am. As a human being, I have my culture and my religion. I do not think that they are the same; it is like night and day, religion and culture. My religion does regulate my life like every other religion, but when somebody asks what am I, I know that I am a Latino. That is the way I feel. It just empowers you to be more Latino. For example, it is funny because I think that out of my whole family, I am the most proud of my roots, at least outwardly. I do not know about inwardly, but outwardly I am probably the proudest to be who I am. So, basically, they could never convince me that I've sold out.

CONVERSION NARRATIVES AS STORIES

While one can find some possible prism through which one can look at these conversion narratives, it is important to recognize that these narratives make "sense only within the framework of the complete life story."[17] In this sense, these conversion narratives should be understood as spiritual life stories, in the way that Elaine J. Lawless speaks about it.[18] In her work with Pentecostal women narratives, Lawless finds that "stories are creations; they cannot be viewed as *pure history*."[19] Further, she acknowledges that looking at these narratives as spiritual life stories allows us to see the actual stories "not perfected entities, but rather each is a collection, a pastiche of stories, many of them based on both personal experience

17. van Nieuwkerk, "Gender, Conversion, and Islam," 95.

18. Lawless, "Rescripting," 53–71.

19. Ibid., 58.

and traditional expectations at the same time."[20] The previous conversion narratives need to be read in light of both the personal experiences and the expectations. The individuals interviewed take several experiences in their lives and put them together in order to tell a story. Narrating these stories provides U.S. Latina/o Muslims with the opportunity of understanding their spiritual trajectory, locating themselves as actors within that story. In this sense, following Lawless' argument, these individuals are "creators" of a story. This narration is not a mere act of "memorization put into words," because the narrative is constructed as it is being told. The process of tying the moments together in order to create a coherent story is actually based on the expectations the individual have regarding the result of the interview. The individuals engage in a process of remembering their life story in light of the audience and the reasons why they are remembering. Then, they put together these life stories that are not about the information but about how the information and their experiences make sense and offer new perspectives. For example, it is important to mention that my own identity as a U.S. Latino non-Muslim interviewer may have affected the way my interviewees construct their narratives and their intent in offering their narratives. Some may have seen this opportunity to tell their story as a mode of *da'wah* towards me, while others may have seen it as way to explain aloud their transformation as part of their path in life, not as a radical change.[21] Thus, their expectations of the conversation and the project guided their narratives.

At the same time, since all but one of the interviews were held in groups, their stories incorporate the perspectives of other members of the community as they compare and contrast their conversion experiences with others. Even if the individual stories are different, the narrating turns into a community activity as people start to remember together. This means that the conversion narratives, as spiritual life stories, "illustrate the collaborative aspects of community-shared narrative."[22] These narratives speak then not only to their personal transformation but also to the connection between their transformation and their social location, which allow us to understand how U.S. Latina/o Muslims build a community and at same time how they see themselves within the larger population.

20. Ibid., 58–59.

21. The latter is probably the one I observed the most in my fieldwork.

22. Lawless, 60.

U.S. Latina/o Muslims see the sharing of their story as an opportunity to show that their conversion should not be understood outside of their Latina/o identity but as part of it, and the narrative is a form of proving this aspect. Telling a story becomes a strategy by which to confront the perspectives and stereotypes that have been constructed by those outside this community. Hence, individuals in their narrating may seem to be responding not only to the general questions I asked, but also to specific concerns they have heard from other members of society, family members, and friends as well as the media. Conversion narratives, in this instance, become a vehicle through which U.S. Latina/o Muslims enter the public discussion and then challenge the common understandings of what it means to be a U.S. Latina/o.[23]

Coming from outside of the common understandings of what it means to be a U.S. Latina/o (e.g. Catholic or at least Christian), these spiritual life stories acquire a marginalized character that functions as a counter-discourse, even if the individual narrating them does not see himor herself as engaging in subversive activity. The fact is that by narrating about their conversion process and reflecting upon it, U.S. Latina/o Muslims are engaged in the re-construction of their identities, which, in many senses, as we will explore in the next chapters, challenge those common understandings. In this regard, I agree with philosopher Shari Stone-Mediatore, who in her analysis of stories from marginalized experiences finds "that such stories, precisely by virtue of their artful and engaged elements, can respond to inchoate, contradictory, unpredictable aspects of historical experience and can thereby destabilize ossified truths and foster critical inquiry into the uncertainties and complexities of historical life."[24] The material embedded within these stories brings forth new information (or a re-thinking of established information) that questions and/or expands the defined histories and projects (identity) and recasts categories. Outside of a few newspaper articles and some articles in magazines, the story about U.S. Latina/o Muslims has been relegated to the margins, so it is through these narratives, these creations, that the story(ies) acquire a new public role, which serves: 1) other U.S. Latina/o Muslims in their quest to build a strong community and identities; 2) non-Muslim U.S. Latina/os in their pursuit to understand this not as mere phenomenon

---

23. For a deeper understanding on how storytelling from marginalized experiences serve as a form of resistance, see Stone-Mediatore, *Reading Across Borders*.

24. Stone-Mediatore, *Reading Across Borders*, 9.

but as part of the larger community; and 3) scholars who try to look at how these stories alter the common understandings of what it means to be a U.S. Latina/o, rather than seeing that as constituting just one fixed thing.

Of course it is important to acknowledge that we are not forgetting the limits inherent in these narratives, which can seem to be introducing a "construction of history and confusing it with history per se."[25] But, at the same time, through these life stories, "we must risk narrating our world, for only when we narrate historical phenomena can we not merely passively endure them but (at least begin to) thoughtfully and collectively confront them."[26] This applies to every attempt at constructing a historical representation, as all of them are limited by the social location of the person doing the construction and do not replace the information gathered from theory and analysis. But, as Stone-Mediatore recognizes, even with these limitations, and not denying them, stories that come from marginalized experiences serve an important purpose. She states, "Such stories do not substitute for theory or empirical data; however, when stories use language creatively to throw new light on familiar worlds, when they explore possible ways to assimilate strange phenomena within our historical imagination, and when they give coherence, albeit a tentative, open-ended coherence, to unique historical phenomena, stories achieve what theory and data cannot."[27] It is in this way that these narratives help us understand the process through which U.S. Latina/o Muslims not only convert but also how identities are re-constructed after conversion.

25. Ibid., 44.
26. Ibid.
27. Ibid., 45.

2

Finding Enlightenment: Journey to Islam

THE CONVERSION NARRATIVES INTRODUCED in the previous chapter (and those not included), while not homogenous, still contain an important aspect that actually ties them together: the converts see their conversion as a process and not a simple event. Indeed, most of them explain life story in terms of this process of conversion to Islam. So, in order to understand how conversion provides an opportunity to re-construct identities, it is important first to comprehend the conversion process. In this chapter I therefore explore the conversion process among Latina/o Muslims in the United States and its different stages.

CONVERSION TO ISLAM[1]

Growing up, I remember talking about (Christian) conversion as an event, a particular decision an individual makes. But van Nieuwkerk makes the case that, "Conversion takes place in several stages and is usually experienced as a substantial transformation of religious, social, and cultural aspects of daily life."[2] In this sense, conversions to Islam should not be understood as a particular event, even when there is an actual moment when the convert officially becomes a member of the religion (*shahadah*). "Conversion to Islam is embodied through taking up new bodily practices pertaining to praying, fasting, and food. In addition, important markers of identity are often changed, such as the name and appearance, including *hijab* or occasionally *niqab*."[3] U.S. Latina/os who convert to Islam,

1. While I will be referring to the term conversion, "It must be stressed that there is no such word as conversion in the Arabic language; rather, the emphasis is on the idea of becoming a Muslim, that is, 'submitting' to God in the form prescribed by his final revelation." [Jawad, "Female Conversion to Islam," 154.]

2. van Nieuwkerk, "Gender and Conversion to Islam in the West," 4.

3. Ibid.

thus, go through a process that cannot be explained as a simple change of religion.

Conversions to Islam are unlike many conversions within Christianity, specifically Protestantism, whose focus is on an event that took place at a particular place and time. They don't fit within "the Pauline paradigm of sudden, dramatic change," which "combines notions of an unexpected flash of revelation, a radical reversal of previous beliefs and allegiances, and an underlying assumption that converts are passive respondents to outside forces."[4] U.S. Latina/o Muslims speak about their conversion—or reversion—as a process of being involved in an active search.[5] This search takes many forms and every path is different. "This warns us not to essentialize Islam [or conversion to Islam], but to systematically analyze whatever elements of Islam have to offer diverse groups of converts at different times."[6] The coming to Islam for these individuals is a path, a movement towards something new.

There are multiple reasons to explain why individuals, in this case U.S. Latina/os, convert to Islam. The different motives for conversion that Islamist Yvonne Yazbeck Haddad identifies in U.S. American women range from "intellectual connection to Islam," to individuals being "captured by the Qur'an," to a reaction "to the negative experiences the converts had had with Christianity."[7] In the pages that follow, we will see that U.S. Latina/os Muslims use these same motives to explain their conversions, and that they likewise speak of their about it in term of a process.

In their article "Converting: Stages of Religious Change," Lewis R. Rambo and Charles E. Farhadian propose that since "converting is a process, a stage model is useful in portraying phases of a process that takes place over time."[8] This stage model is constituted by seven phases, and while I agree with the authors that, "this stage model must not be seen either as unilinear or as universal," the model does nonetheless help us understand the process of conversion in a more organized way.[9] The first stage, *context*, speaks to the environment and setting where conversion

4. Rambo, "Anthropology and the Study of Conversion," 213.

5. In the next chapter, I examine the concept of reversion and how it serves to explain U.S. Latina/o Muslims' search for identity.

6. van Nieuwkerk, "Gender and Conversion to Islam in the West," 7.

7. Haddad, "The Quest for Peace," 28–29.

8. Rambo and Farhadian, "Converting," 23.

9. Ibid., 24.

happens. This is followed by the *crisis*, which is characterized by those events or experiences that create displacement. The third stage, *quest*, is a response to that crisis as it becomes a search to find locality and meaning. This search is followed by an *encounter* stage, which is defined by the contact with a person who advocates a particular view that can help in the *quest* for meaning. This *encounter* acquires meaning as the *interaction* stage starts and the potential convert begins to relate to this newfound religion in order to get ready to re-construct his/her identity. This reconstruction leads to the *commitment* stage in which the convert chooses to fully accept the new religious ideals, being aware or not of the last stage, *consequences*, which measure the effect of the decision within the particular social location of the convert.

Though this type of model does indeed help us analyze the process of conversion, in order to examine the multiple narratives of conversion by U.S. Latina/o Muslims I make some minor changes to it that I feel are necessary. In particular, the *quest* follows an *encounter* and not the other way around, as it is because of an *encounter* that individuals begin a *quest*. In light of this, *interaction* becomes another aspect of that *quest*, so I do not see it as a separate phase. With such changes in mind, in the next pages I address these stages as I analyze the process of conversion among U.S. Latina/o Muslims.

Context

There is no one particular context that serves as background to explain the bulk of the conversions to Islam since the individuals live not only in different places but also within multiple social contexts. Some people are school, some work, and others are part of the military. But there are three particular characteristics that are important to highlight because while they are not universal they indeed help us understand the general contexts in which these conversions happen. First, within my research I encountered individuals of many different ages, but of these many shared the perspective of an urban setting during the period when they entered a process of conversion. This setting generates the spaces where there is a higher contact and exchange between multiple cultures and religions, so individuals are more exposed to this diversity. Besides the fact that the larger U.S. Latina/o communities are in urban settings, this aspect of urbanization helps explain why is it that the larger U.S. Latina/o Muslim communities can be found in metropolitan areas.

The second aspect that facilitates the understanding of a general context is the Christian background (mostly Catholic, in the cases I document here). This milieu is critical because it has established a particular mentality within the members of this community about their religious identities. It is in contrast to this mentality that converts evaluate their process of conversion. Their new religious experience is compared with this Christian setting and in many cases it is disenchantment with this milieu that prompts them to seek a new religious experience.

Third, the function of movement should be recognized as an important aspect of the context. By movement, I am not just referring to the immigration issue, even though that is obviously a central aspect of it; I also wish to highlight the aspect of constant movement by U.S. Latina/os within their own city, or across states. Two major issues force these movements: family and work. As we saw in Pedro's and Laura's stories, among others, U.S. Latina/os move to visit family, to find work and/or to start a new life. This situation may create some instability in a person's life and this in turn can open the door for considering new perspectives, like a new religion.

Crisis (Spiritual Anomie)

Sonia, one of the interviewees we met in the previous chapter and a U.S. Latina Muslim residing in Chicago, explains that she was Catholic, "*muy católica*" (very Catholic), and that after high school she entered a convent in order to become a nun.[10] After some months in the convent, she found herself more lost than before she entered, disenchanted not only with the convent, but also with the Church and its doctrines. She remembers that she asked the priest many times about the Trinity and other mysteries within Catholicism and that not only did she get no particular concrete answer, but the priest also told her to accept the religion without questioning it. Sonia looks back at that time as her *crisis*. Rambo and Farhadian refer to this stage as a "catalyst for change" as it forces the individual to look for something new.[11] A *crisis* develops from those experiences that disrupt the individual's status quo. In the case of U.S. Latina/o Muslims, as

10. Interview with a group of U.S. Latinas in Chicago (July 26, 2006).
11. Rambo and Farhadian, 25.

in the case of Sonia, *crisis* is often identified by a sense of disenchantment that leads to spiritual anomie. Spiritual anomie refers to the feeling of an individual (or group) who can find neither tangible nor existential answers within her/his religious group, and this generates not merely doubts and suspicion, but mostly a lack of meaning. People express this spiritual anomie through doubt regarding religious ideas and 'mysteries,' as well as through abandoning religious institutions.

Most U.S. Latina/os who convert to Islam experience this type of disenchantment because while they sought concrete answers to questions about theological issues, they were often "troubled by confusing and complicated theological notions in Christianity."[12] They feel that Christianity, mainly Catholicism, and its leaders have not been able to address "the perennial doctrines that have set the two faiths apart: the concepts of incarnation and Trinity, the divinity of Jesus, crucifixion, and the doctrine of original sin."[13] In the same way, reporter Chris L. Jenkins observes, "Many of the converts say they are choosing Islam because they feel the religion gives them greater direct contact with God, without saints and a rigid church hierarchy."[14] Rosa, a U.S. Latina Muslim also from Chicago, points to this disenchantment as the initial stage in her conversion. In particular she recalls doubting what her family, the priests, and the nuns told her regarding Jesus and the Trinity. She did not understand the concepts explained to her about Catholicism, but kept getting the same answers that focused principally on the relationship between Mexican identity and Catholicism. Rosa felt that she was expected to believe just because she was Mexican, not for any logical reason, and with time she felt she did not belong to that community, as those beliefs were ones she did not share. During this period she used to think, "*No sabía donde cabía*" (I did not know where I did fit).[15] Iris, another U.S. Latina Muslim in Chicago, also felt she needed to be Catholic because she was Mexican. In her interview, she expressed that for a long time she thought of herself as a Catholic for the "logic" of it: Mexicans are Catholics, she is Mexican, and consequently she is Catholic. But, like Rosa, she had many questions regarding the religion of her parents. She couldn't understand and resisted the idea of

---

12. Haddad, 30.

13. Ibid., 29–30.

14. Jenkins, "Islam Luring More Latinos," para. 7.

15. Interview with a group of U.S. Latinas in Chicago (July 26, 2006).

mysteries; that, combined with the lack of satisfying answers from church leaders, led her to abandon the church in her teenage years.

It is not only dissatisfaction with Catholicism that my interviewees reported, but also spiritual anomie within other religious institutions or systems. For example, Pedro, a U.S. Latino Muslim from Los Angeles, explains that he went from Catholicism to Native American religion in search of answers that these religious systems did not have, and that this in time led him to Islam.[16] Laura, a woman residing in Chicago, found herself experiencing spiritual anomie as she pondered the ideas pre-sented to her by her father, a Pentecostal pastor.[17] She had many doubts regarding what she calls the "myths and realities" of the Bible and the truth about miracles, which led her to feel disappointed with the beliefs she had been taught as a child. She was blunt in our discussion, saying, "*Me sentía vacía*" (I felt empty). So both of these examples fit with the other ones mentioned before as they show that the feeling of dislocation created by a *crisis* is what triggers the search for a new system. As Rambo and Farhadian state, "Crises are disordering and disrupting experiences that call into question a person's or group's taken-for-granted world."[18] In the case of U.S. Latina/o Muslims, these crises are not determined by a particular set of actions or events but by the deep sense of disillusion these individuals have with their spiritual identity. The sense of spiritual anomie makes these individuals open to the possibility something new.

Encounter (Contact and Exchange)

After leaving the convent and visiting a Pentecostal church, Sonia started to work in a department store in Manhattan, where she lived at the time. Most of her fellow employees at the store were Muslims and with that contact and exchange, Sonia became interested in learning more about Islam. Sonia's story is not uncommon; many U.S. Latina/os have their first *encounter* with Islam through their workplace. For example, Elena and Carol, two U.S. Latinas residing in Los Angeles, learned about Islam from Muslim colleagues in their respective jobs. This type of encounter represents the typical first contact most U.S. Latina/o Muslims describe as they narrate their conversion stories. For the most part, the encounter

16. Interview with a group of U.S. Latina/os in Los Angeles (July 28, 2006).

17. Interview with a group of U.S. Latinas in Chicago (July 26, 2006).

18. Rambo and Farhadian, 25.

with a co-worker, a friend, or a family member who invites them to read the Qur'an and learn about Islam becomes the initial proactive phase in the process of conversion. These encounters should be seen as part of the *da'wah* in which Muslims are always engaged. Yvonne Yazbeck Haddad explains the importance of the encounters arguing that, "While the articulation of Islam and its teaching for Westerners is important in appealing to seekers, crucial for many of the converts were their initial encounters with Muslims—friends, classmates, boyfriends, spouses, acquaintances, and neighbors who took the time and had the patience to explain, to mentor and guide."[19] For the most part, these encounters take place in private settings and not as part of some public proselytizing activity—which is not to say that the encounters are not in some way proselytizing actions.[20] The private setting of these contacts becomes the essential aspect of this stage as these interactions happen usually through close-knit relations, and sometimes through one-on-one relations.

Pedro, after five years of practicing Native American religions, was introduced to Islam through a friend, who put him in contact with the Qur'an. In the same way, Rosa had her first encounter with Islam through her neighbor and best friend in high school. Her relationship with her friend became that first link that put her on the path to finding answers to her questions. These stories exemplify the way most U.S. Latina/o Muslims have their encounters with friends. For example, in my conversation with a group of U.S. Latina/o Muslims in the Bay Area, I found that six out of the seven identify a friend as the person that triggered their move towards Islam.[21] For most of them, these contacts became companions in the conversion process, so it was not just a particular contact without exchange. Relationships were established or strengthened after these encounters, and became essential aspects of the process. Felix explains that he "got exposed to Islam while he was in high school from a Bolivian friend," and

---

19. Haddad, 27.

20. While the process of conversion to Islam is dissimilar to Protestant conversions, I can easily see similarities within the two groups. For example, the enthusiasm and effort both of these groups put into proselytizing is comparable, although U.S. Latina/o Muslims do not consider their effort proselytizing but *da'wah*, the process through which Muslims educate others about Islam.

21. Interview with members of Latino Muslims of the Bay Area, in Hayward, California (July 30, 2006).

that this friend "was very influential" in his life.[22] This relationship represented an intimate contact that provoked change. Rafael, also from the Bay Area, likewise describes his initial encounter with Islam as a personal contact with a friend, whom he knew before he became Muslim and continued to see afterwards. Rafael remembers that his friend would invite him to his house as he did before he converted but now he would tell him stories from the Sira. This exchange made the difference in Rafael's life as he moved towards Islam.

As mentioned above, some of these encounters also happened among family members, which in most cases increases the significance of the contact. Laura, as well as Iris, another U.S. Latina I met with in Chicago, came to Islam after an encounter with men whom they later married.[23] Iris' case is particularly interesting; she then became a contact person herself for her family, especially her mother, who was also present during our conversation in Chicago. Marta, Iris' mother, remembers that she was really worried when her daughter first told her about her decision to convert to Islam because she feared her daughter was not going to attain salvation. As a Catholic, Marta thought that she was responsible not only for her own salvation but for that of her family as well. She recalls that it was Iris who actually calmed her down and told her: "Mami, por favor no digas nada y no me discutas, sólo lea el Corán primero" (Mom, please do not tell me anything and don't argue, just read the Qur'an first).[24] For Marta, this encounter acquired significance because it was her daughter Iris making that contact and she witnessed the transformation in Iris' life. From that moment on, Marta, like many other U.S. Latina/o Muslims after their encounter, began an examination of Islam, "a quest for knowledge or spiritual fulfillment."[25]

22. Ibid.

23. While we will address the issue of gender and Latinas' conversions later in the chapter, it is important here to state that while it is not uncommon to find U.S. Latinas who marry Muslim men and because of that contact convert to Islam, this is not the norm.

24. Interview with a group of U.S. Latinas in Chicago (July 26, 2006).

25. Haddad, 27.

Quest (Search)

Marta followed her daughter's advice and started to read the Qur'an, or, as she puts it, "No lo leí, me lo bebí" (I did not read it, I drank it).[26] She read it everyday until she was done with it and this provoked a process of searching. Through this search, she became an active participant in a *quest* as she sought "to maximize meaning and purpose in life."[27] After the encounter, U.S. Latina/o Muslims speak about a period when they not only read the Qur'an but also start studying about Islam through reading other materials and especially through conversation with Muslims—in other words, through both personal and communal actions. It is because of this period of searching that conversions to Islam are considered "primarily intellectual" when compared to the emotional aspect of Christian conversions.[28] But, this consideration doesn't do justice to the actual spiritual engagement within the quest. Islamist Yasin Dutton argues that this is one of the most difficult things to address because there is a tendency to argue, "that Islam appeals by its 'rationality' and that an unbiased study of the texts will – or should in theory – lead to the reader becoming Muslim."[29] For U.S. Latina/o Muslims, it is important to address the spiritual character of their conversion because while they speak of the rational aspects of their decision, most maintain that it was "by a recognition of the heart."[30]

María, a Puerto Rican woman in New York, stated that, "Now, I am a pretty analytical person so it is not like I heard the verses of the Qur'an and all of a sudden I started to convert. I mean that happens to a lot of people and that is beautiful, but that did not happen to me."[31] She talked about her conversion as an analytical process, explaining the process to me like this: "I was continuously researching, but it was a research that I could not put away. Even at times, I would put the materials away, and I would say: "Forget this, I have other things to do." Within a couple of days it was like I had to go back to it, a project I had to continue to finish it."[32] Thus, for María, and most U.S. Latina/o Muslims, the quest is not just an

---

26. Ibid.

27. Rambo and Farhadian, 27.

28. Sánchez and Galván, "Latino Muslims," 25.

29. Dutton, "Conversion to Islam," 163.

30. Ibid.

31. Interview with María in New York City (July 23, 2006).

32. Ibid.

academic or intellectual enterprise, but also a fundamentally spiritual one. While none of the interviewees spoke about Sufism, the way that some U.S. Latina/o Muslims speak about the spiritual aspect of conversion resembles a conversion to Sufism, which is considered to be the mystical dimension of Islam. This should not be any surprise since research indicates, "that Sufism is the main agent for conversion to Islam in the West."[33] This spiritual aspect is important because it defines the individual's search in light of the *crisis*. Most U.S. Latina/o Muslims identify their quest as the period of learning and education, on that often takes a considerable amount of time. In my research, for example, the length of this quest phase varied from six months to two years among those I interviewed. Converts take this time to look for answers to the issues that caused their crisis in the first place. After leaving the convent and having an encounter with Muslims in her workplace, Sonia started not only researching the different aspects of Islam but also going to the Centro Islámico in New York and taking classes about Islam. What most attracted her to Islam was "la parte espiritual" (the spiritual part), and it was this feature that shaped her search.[34] In that search, she found it particularly engaging to be asked to research the topics herself and not just believe because the teacher told her to. Such serious inquiry is what most U.S. Latina/o Muslims see as attractive and why the quest itself is essential.

Rosa started her quest by talking to Muslims whenever she met one. She would talk to them about the role of prayer and issues dealing with family, as these were important for her. Interestingly, after this continuous search it was when she bought a copy of the Qur'an, and in her words once she started reading, ". . . yo no sé cómo explicarlo, lo que sentí, por que era como me estaba hablando" (I do not know how to explain it, what I felt it was like was that it was talking to me).[35] Rosa felt her questions and doubts were being answered. Her process underscores not only the merging of an intellectual aspect and a spiritual element within this quest, it also highlights the centrality of addressing the crisis as the search develops.

---

33. van Nieuwkerk, "Gender and Conversion to Islam in the West," 5. For a comprehensive understanding of the Sufi appeal, especially for women, see Jawad, "Female Conversion to Islam," 153–71.

34. Interview with a group of U.S. Latinas in Chicago (July 26, 2006).

35. Ibid.

Elena, after her encounter with Muslims co-workers, started to read and research about Islam and then progressed to talking to Muslims and especially an Imam. She reports that her intention in starting to read was never to become a Muslim; she was simply interested in learning why women wear a *hijab* or why men have multiple wives. But the more she learned, the more she found herself wanting to know, so she started having conversations with an imam, and even participated in Sunday classes at the *masjid* or mosque). Elena was so deeply engaged in this *quest* that as she learned more and her questions were being answered, she felt "like a Muslim" even though she had not officially taken the *shahadah* (declaration of faith).[36] In the same way, Carol, after her conversation with Muslim friends and her study of the Qur'an and other books, found answers to her questions. She always questioned the multiple definitions regarding Jesus being God and human at the same time, which she recognizes "didn't really click," as a Catholic.[37] Carol's reaction is not unique; many U.S. Latina/o Muslims speak of Islam as a system that answer their questions. And yet I also agree with Haddad's understanding of Muslims' conversion narratives when she argues that,

> There appears to be little awareness among the converts who have posted or published their conversion narratives of the development of Islamic thought and its rich history intellectual debates. The conversion narratives lack any reference to intellectual challenges that Islam has not been able to resolve or questions that have not been answered. The texts they read are self-assured and persuasive. Many remarked that Islam was more pure than Christianity and less influenced by humans.[38]

While it may seem romantic, this understanding of Islam suggests that these converts are in a process of searching and that this religion offered them some answers. It may be that in the future, after more research, they come to a more critical understanding of Islam but for now this understanding of Islam addresses their spiritual frustration. Through this perspective they encounter the new religious experience and commit to a new religious system.

---

36. Interview with a group of U.S. Latina/os in Los Angeles (July 28, 2006).

37. Ibid.

38. Haddad, 30.

Commitment (Shahadah)

Once individuals find their way out of their spiritual anomie, they are ready to make a formal decision for a particular religious system, a *commitment*. As Lewis Rambo states, "commitment is the consummation of the conversion process," and it "empowers the convert with a sense of connection with God and the community."[39] Those converting to Islam affirm their commitment by taking the *shahadah,* which consists of a public declaration of faith "in front of witnesses."[40] U.S. Latina/o Muslims make this *commitment* after a long quest, but the ways these decisions are made do not reflect one particular paradigm. On the contrary, most, if not all, of the individuals I encountered in my research talked about the *shahadah* as something that they needed to do, but they did not all follow the same process to arrive there. As they tell it, it just happened one day. For example, Carol took the *shahadah* one day without actually planning on it. Ramadan was coming and Carol wanted to participate in the fasting and the people at the *masjid* told her that because she was not yet a Muslim, she could not participate. At that moment, she decided to officially convert and take the *shahadah* in front of the other members of the class. Though this may sound like an impulsive decision, it was in fact the culmination of her search. Yet the commitment to Islam involves more than the ritual of taking the *shahadah.*

After conversion, "it is expected that anyone entering Islam will neither drink alcohol nor eat pork or meat of any incorrectly slaughtered animal, and will respect the basic prohibitions relating to such matters as stealing, committing adultery and/or fornication, murder, and so on."[41] At the same time, there is an expectation that individuals will adopt a Muslim name, participate "in transformative rites such as a Muslim pilgrimage to Mecca," and/or, for women in particular, they should wear "particular clothes."[42] These expectations played out in different ways and at different times among converts. For example, people often adopt dietary restrictions as a first response to conversion and later change their name, and yet later plan a pilgrimage. For women, wearing the *hijab* (head covering) is an important step, and one unique to women; male converts do not

---

39. Rambo, *Understanding Religious Conversion*, 168–69.

40. Dutton, 154.

41. Ibid., 155–56.

42. Rambo and Farhadian, 32.

have to so quickly and publicly make known their decision. As Haddad points out, "Consistently the *hijab* seemed to be a bigger issue for families and friends than the conversion itself," since "This visible display of Islam was seen as too radical," and their "Family members were often concerned about what neighbors and other people would think about the change in wardrobe."[43]

U.S. Latinas who convert to Islam are aware of what will be expected of them as Muslim women, and these issues are part of their search and decision-making process before taking the *shahadah*. Most Latinas I interviewed not only talked to other Muslim women but also observed the interaction between men and women and saw something different from their own social reality. At the same time, as Karin van Nieuwkerk finds, "female conversions [compared to those of males] may raise even stronger reactions because traditions have often constructed women as symbols of ethnic and religious boundaries."[44] These attitudes are exemplified in the common discourses about Islam and its treatment of women, especially in the last few years with the development of the so-called "war on terror." The discourse about the liberation of women as it pertains to some communities in the Middle East (e.g. Afghanistan under the control of the Taliban) has becomes the normative discourse and perceives Islam "as relegating women to subservience, second-class status, a polygamous environment, and physical and sexual abuse."[45] Because of these constructions about womanhood, U.S. Latina Muslims are usually judged for their conversion and often are "regularly treated with hostility."[46] And yet for many of them the differences between their cultural construction and the perspective of their newfound religion regarding the treatment of women are essential to how they explain their conversion. For example, many women mentioned machismo, which their culture and Christianity promote, as something they do not like within their U.S. Latino tradition.

While pointing out that there are many cultural similarities between Latino culture and Arabic/Muslim culture, María argues that one of the important aspects she found in her quest is that women within Islam are not blamed for men's sin, as is often the case in Christians' interpreta-

---

43. Haddad, 31.

44. van Nieuwkerk, "Gender and Conversion to Islam in the West," 1.

45. Haddad, 20.

46. van Nieuwkerk, "Gender and Conversion to Islam in the West," 1.

tion of the creation narrative. María found that in Islam, "Everyone is responsible for their own actions and responsible for their own sin, and it is interesting that in Islam, people are responsible for their worship and their prayers. Men and women are equally responsible. In Christianity, a woman is responsible for everything and yet she can also be told what to do since she is seen as being beneath a man. Islam is different in that way. Christianity is so engraved in our minds that one does not seem to question that sort of injustice."[47] For her, this was a stark difference from what she had experienced in Christianity and it allowed her to look at herself differently as a woman, not as someone beneath men but equal to men. This understanding of responsibility and equality is often what encourages María, and other U.S. Latinas, to engage with the issues of head covering and other expectations for women within Islam. They see it as a responsibility to God, not to men.

In my conversation with María, she spoke frankly about wearing the *hijab*. Rather than considering it oppressive, she feels it illustrates women's responsibility and freedom. Women wear the *hijab* because God—not men—says they have to wear it. Thus, this expectation becomes a decision, not an imposition. Furthermore, many women argue that the wearing of the *hijab* highlights their break with the materialistic aspects of society. María mentioned that by wearing the *hijab* she feels freed from judgments of her beauty, which for many people has to do with one's hair. Laura goes even further, saying that the issue of modesty was one of the important things that attracted her to Islam. She recalls as a non-Muslim often going shopping to keep up with the latest fashions, but says she was attracted to the emphasis on the spiritual rather than material aspects of life in Islam. While others pay attention to accessories and style, she can concentrate on prayer. These liberating perspectives regarding the wearing of the *hijab* and the dress code within Islam typify the general sentiment of U.S. Latina Muslims, although it is true that many within the larger U.S. Latino community see them as oppressive, because of the "patterns of sexuality in Western society and the emphasis on the packaging of the female body and its appearance."[48]

---

47. Interview with María in New York City (July 23, 2006).

48. Haddad, 35. This reminds me about one of the first times I heard a Muslim women talk about the *hijab*. In an academic meeting in Canada, a Canadian Muslim women who was presenting a paper was asked if she found that wearing the *hijab* was oppressive, and she calmly responded that waking up in the morning thinking about what to wear and

The larger U.S. Latino community's view of Islam can represent a challenge to those who consider converting. This challenge is part of the *consequences* of taking the *shahadah*. Since U.S. Latina/o Muslims become aware of these issues during their *quest*, they are prepared to confront those interpretations and stereotypes that situate Islam as an oppressive religion.

Consequences

The transformations that U.S. Latina/o Muslims go through after conversion not only affect the spiritual aspects of their lives, but also their relationship with others, especially with their family and those within the U.S. Latino community. While the spiritual side is usually developed through prayer and conversation with the imam and other members of the religious community, the reactions of family and friends of the convert tends to characterize the way the convert re-defines her/his own identity. Most U.S. Latina/o Muslims experience challenges (questioning, confrontation, even ridicule) from the larger U.S. Latino community because of what it considers radical changes in lifestyle. They are seen, in many cases, as losing their culture and *latinidad*, their Latino/a identity. Hence, these individuals find themselves as outsiders within their own community, or as Michelle Al-Nasr states:

> Becoming estranged to the same people that you have known all your living years. All of the sudden, you are the outcast, the lost soul who doesn't have enough sense to know what you are doing, everyone is telling you that you are throwing your entire life away.[49]

They have become Other even within their own culture. Public perspectives regarding Islam shape most of the responses by the community and family members.

The events of 9-11 precipitated many derogatory portrayals of Islam, and therefore of Muslims. Despite the negative stereotypes, many

---

what make-up to use in order to impress is the oppressive system. For her, not following Western conceptions of beauty was liberatory. When I shared this story with the group of U.S. Latina Muslims in Chicago, all of them agree full-heartedly. For a broad analysis on the meanings of the use of the *hijab*, see Allievi, "The Shifting," 120–49. For a perspective from a U.S. Latina Muslim see Sánchez, "An Answer: Why Muslim Women Cover," no pages.

49. Al-Nasr, "A Letter to my Family," para. 3.

U.S. Latina/o Muslims say that this very publicity and their fascination with Islam were the main reasons they began researching and learning about it. Eventually, many found themselves taking the *shahadah*, and the U.S. Latina/o Muslim community began to grow steadily even within this tense atmosphere. Despite this growth in U.S. Latina/o conversions to Islam, negative portrayals of Islam and Muslims did not cease in the Spanish-speaking media. The broadcast of the Brazilian *tele-novela El Clon* serves as an example. This, "the highest-rated soap opera ever shown on Telemundo," not only had a Muslim character as the main character who was portrayed in a negative light, but also offered "a profusion of Orientalist imagery."[50] It portrayed an Islamic world based upon the traditional negative stereotypes, which were so problematic that,

> [t]he Moroccan ambassador to Brazil, in a letter to a Sao Paolo newspaper, criticized the series for its egregious "cultural errors," "gross falsification" and "mediocre images" promoting stereotypes of Muslim women as submissive and men as polygamists leading lives of "luxury and indolence."[51]

Spanish-speaking television thus reinforced mainstream discourse that constructed Muslims as Other, and U.S. Latino communities bought into these ideas.

Another example of the prevalence of this stereotypical view within Spanish-speaking media is the airing of "El Show de Cristina" on December 17, 2001 called "Behind the Veil," which portrayed Islam in a negative way, specifically regarding its "mistreatment" of women. Yet, no U.S. Latina Muslim was invited to present her view on the topic, and this led Khadija Rivera and a group of U.S. Latina Muslims to write an online petition, signed by hundreds of people, against this type of misrepresentation.[52] Most U.S. Latina/o Muslims, along with Saraji Umm Zaid, believe that "Spanish speaking television has done Islam a grave disservice with numerous shows promoting the old 'Islam is terror and oppresses women' view."[53]

The media's stereotyping and misrepresentations advanced the prejudice and marginalization of U.S. Latina/o Muslims within the Latino

---

50. Aidi, "Let Us Be Moors," para. 12.
51. Ibid.
52. Parodi et al., "Petition to Protest," no pages.
53. Zaid, "Latinos, Islam, and New York City," para. 4.

community in the United States. They are looked at with distrust, especially from the older generation of Latina/os in the United States. While certainly many families respect a member's decision to convert, most U.S. Latina/o Muslims have to contend with suspicious responses from society. The responses of those closest to the convert vary considerably; some are extremely supportive while others totally marginalize the convert, often simply buying into well-worn stereotypes. For example, the experience of Iris and Marta, in which the daughter's conversion led to the mother's, while not uncommon, only portrays one aspect of the consequences U.S. Latina/o Muslims deal with after conversion within their family.

"¡Santísimo! ¿Y qué es lo que le pasa a esta muchacha?" (Holy! What is wrong with this youngster?)[54] These were the words Sonia heard her dad say the first time she came out of her room wearing her *hijab*. Her mother instantly stopped him and said: "No, déjala, que eso se le va a pasar" (No, leave her alone as that will go away).[55] Well, "it" did not go away, but as time went by, while still not totally on board with the change, her family did become accustomed to the idea of Sonia's conversion. For Sonia, the turning point came during her first celebration of Ramadan. When her family saw her fasting, they became much more conscious of her commitment and were so respectful that they would not allow anybody to eat in front of her. This is the type of experience most of the younger generations of converts speak about. Though at the beginning their family members would typically be surprised and would even make fun of them, after some time, most of them would realize that it was a decision that transformed their loved one's life for the better.

María related that as she began progressing in her newfound faith and becoming serious in her transformation, her family realized that the good things about her were left intact while the bad things were changing. While this evolution was taking place, she still participated actively in her family life in order to keep lines of communication open and not lose her roots. In many cases, U.S. Latina/os who convert to Islam argue that they work harder than before on their transformation and in the way they conduct their lives in order to prove that they made the right choice, and to respond to their family and friends' initial reaction of incredulity and suspicion. This was the case for Marta, who after conversion felt obliged

---

54. Interview with a group of U.S. Latinas in Chicago (July 26, 2006).
55. Ibid.

always to do the right thing, especially since her in-laws were not happy with her decision. As Sonia, María, and Marta did, most U.S. Latina/o Muslims become not just examples of what it entails to be Muslim, but teachers to those around them, especially to their families.

Because the negative stereotypes about Islam are so prevalent, converts are always explaining their decision and the truths about their newfound religion in order to repudiate the notion that Islam is about violence and war. Iris remembers that when she went to Mexico to visit her extended family she had to explain why she wore a *hijab* because most of her family members jumped to the conclusion that wearing a *hijab* was an oppressive activity. To this accusation she responded by establishing that the decision to wear it was based on modesty and that it was not any different from the old Christian tradition of head covering. This type of exchange is common between converts and their family members right after the conversion and typically the outcome of the conversation determines to what extent the family will support or reject the convert. In Iris's case, after some time she felt support from her family in Mexico because they saw her transformation as something good. But not all families are so supportive, especially those that see the conversion as an act of disloyalty towards the culture.

In the same way that Rosa and Iris thought that being Catholic was an important and intrinsic aspect of being Mexican, many U.S. Latina/os use this stereotype to critique the conversion. For Samantha, a woman living in Chicago who came to Islam through the Nation of Islam, this idea of culture being tied to a particular religion became central in her father's response to her decision. She remembers how he once told her: "Mi'ja this is our tradition. You know and I know; you'll come back. You'll come back because this is our tradition. And look at everybody, at the whole family, you are going to be an outsider when we go visit the family."[56] Initially, Samantha found resistance with her father and the rest of the family but with time she feels the relationship has become stronger as they search for commonalities while respecting their differences. For somebody like Arturo, a young man from the Bay Area in California who encountered similar resistance from his family, the process was different because his mother was confused and took his conversion "pretty hard."[57] She felt re-

56. Ibid.

57. Interview with members of Latino Muslims of the Bay Area, in Hayward, California (July 30, 2006).

sponsible for Arturo's decision to leave the Catholic Church, blaming herself for not raising him "more Catholic," or for not taking him to church regularly on Sundays. But as in Samantha's case, after some time she and the rest of the family came around to the idea of Arturo's conversion and now support him.

Carol likewise encountered resistance from her family when she told them about her conversion. Her mother and her sister gave her a hard time because of the head covering by arguing that it was ridiculous and made her look ugly. Her father went even further by blaming on her head covering everything bad that happened. Carol mentions that while her family have come around to the idea of her conversion, it is hard to avoid these conversations because members of the extended family and friends of the family continue to criticize her. She is always addressing their concerns but their relationship has improved because there is more openness at least for the conversation to happen.

Others encounter more challenges. Sometimes a family's criticism turns into attacks. Roberto, who first became interested in Islam because of *wudu*, has been engaged in a long process of convincing his family that Islam is not the religion of Satan. He has been called names by family members, including "terrorista, petrolero y talibán" (terrorist, oilman, and Taliban), which, as Roberto relates, created some tense arguments.[58] But the biggest issue came when Roberto decided to change his name to a Muslim name because it was then when his family started accusing him of betrayal. After that he decided to "segregate" himself from his family for some time, and it was not until some of the family members, beginning with his brother, started asking questions without the constant condemnation, that their relationships improved. Now, although they still have their doubts and concerns, there is much more communication within the family; even Roberto's mother stopped believing that Islam is the religion of Satan after Roberto gave her a Qur'an.

Other individuals are forced to be silent and not discuss their new faith with their family members. Yolanda, a young woman from the Bay Area in California who studied for two years before converting to Islam, struggled for a long time to tell her family. Before telling them, she wanted to learn as much as possible in order to be comfortable explaining her decision. Her family "wasn't very happy" when she revealed her decision, and

58. Interview with a group of U.S. Latina/os in Los Angeles (July 28, 2006).

even months after she told them, they still do not want to talk about the situation.[59] She observes that the problem is that they "don't understand about the religion yet," as "they view it from the media's perspective."[60]

Yolanda confronted the same attitude among some friends, so she decided that it was better not say anything. Yolanda's story is not unique. Julio, who also converted after two years of reading the Qur'an and other literature on Islam, while reflecting on his family's reaction to his conversion says: "They told me they don't want to know anything about it. So, I just respected that and we have a good relationship."[61] He reflected upon the situation and reached the conclusion that the principle of "don't ask, don't tell" would be the best way to keep a civil relationship within his household. This is how he lives his life even among friends: he doesn't tell them about his conversion unless they ask him. Sometimes he avoids hanging out with them in order to avoid the conversation and the awkwardness of the situation.

Yolanda and Julio's stories are just two examples of how U.S. Latina/o Muslims struggle. Yolanda and Julio reflect upon all the times they have tried to talk about their decision and are ridiculed, and how they need to teach their friends about Islam in order to achieve respect and common ground. For women it becomes a special challenge; many of their female friends consider their change in dress habits as an imposition and/or as an oppressive activity.

For Rosa, this situation became her daily experience. Her friends were always arguing that while they respect her decision they thought Rosa's physical changes were not the result of her own conviction but because of pressure from her husband—even though she explained that her decision was not made in response to her husband but in response to God. Rosa tried to keep these friends but after a while she realized that the social activities and the drinking were the only things that her friends were interested in doing with her. She felt uncomfortable in these gatherings because drinking was not what she wanted to do. She decided to spend less time with them and, after a while, these friendships lapsed. Now, she has just begun to form friendships with a few Muslims with whom she finds she has more in common. Such changes of friendships

59. Interview with members of Latino Muslims of the Bay Area, in Hayward, California (July 30, 2006).

60. Ibid.

61. Ibid.

are important for U.S. Latina/o Muslims because they define their challenges as part of the *consequences* of conversion. During our conversation in Chicago, after listening to Rosa's story, Kristina, a young U.S. Latina, suddenly said:

> I want to say that yo también, I lost all of my friends. Yeah, all of them because they did not understand. Why are you covering yourself? ¿Por qué no puedes estar aquí si es solo nosotros los que estamos tomando? Y como ella dice (referring to Elena), no me respetaban. Me preguntaba a mi misma, ¿y, por qué ando con esta gente si no me respetan a mí? Yo les respeto a ellos. Y yo decía, estos no son friends, you know because a friend is going to respect you. So I lost all of my friends, but *alhumdillah*, I have wonderful friends now.[62]

While these experiences do not represent the totality of the community, most U.S. Latina/o Muslims do indeed speak about how hard it has been to keep their friends.

BEYOND CONVERSION: FROM LIMINALITY
TO COMMUNITY

The process of conversion to Islam for U.S. Latina/os does not end with taking the *shahadah* and the consequences of doing so. In fact it is often then that the greatest challenges begin. As stated above, U.S. Latina/os have become Others within their communities and families. This otherness can be described as marginality (on the border), as inferiority (less than), or as liminality (in-between).[63] I argue that in order to understand the otherness U.S. Latina/o Muslims confront after conversion, we need to see it as a state of liminality.

To live in a liminal space is to live in-between. Philosopher James C. Conroy argues that, "This liminal position, which sits on the border, is always in a relationship of tension with the political or cultural centre to which it is attached. It is more or less determined by the centre in that the liminal-border position is, inevitably in some significant respects, at

---

62. Interview with a group of U.S. Latinas in Chicago (July 26, 2006). The translation of the parts in Spanish is: "Why can't you be here if we are just the ones drinking? And like she said, they did not respect me. I asked myself, why do I hang out with these people if they don't respect me? I respect them."

63. For a description of these three types of "cultural manifestations," see La Shure, "What is Liminality?," no pages.

odds with the centre position."[64] While not denying the relationship between the liminal space and the centre, what I refer to as the dominant conventional paradigm, I disagree with Conroy's location of liminality as in the border (margins). I agree with Charles La Shure, who, based on an analysis of Victor Turner's work, argues that liminality is "not outside of the social structure or on its edges, it is in the cracks within the social structure itself."[65] This corresponds with Conroy's assessment that "the liminal moment may arise *within* the bounded space of a given society while at the same time not being *off* it."[66] What this means is that U.S. Latina/o Muslims are situated as Others within the larger U.S. Latina/o community, in-between the cracks of the social structure, not at the margins of it. They are not culturally ignorant about U.S. Latina/os as they are members of the larger structure, but their decision to convert puts them at odds with the dominant conventional constructions (or centre) of U.S. Latina/o culture and identities. This "contradictory" path thus locates them in those in-between spaces of being and not being, isolated within the community, as I have shown before.

On the other hand, the condition of liminality for U.S. Latina/o Muslims is not limited to their location within the U.S. Latina/o community but also within the larger U.S. Muslim community. U.S. Latina/o Muslims point out that they have encountered some isolation from non-Latina/o Muslims because they are seen as outsiders. U.S. Latina/os, because of cultural stereotypes about the community such as drinking and adultery, are seen as incapable of being good Muslims. The larger Muslim community doubts the authenticity of their conversion. While I did not hear any major complaint about this in my interviews (no question was specifically directed to such issues), such responses have been documented. For example, Aziz, a U.S. Latino Muslim interviewed by Juan Galván, executive director of the Latin American Da'wah Organization (LADO), explains: "One of the biggest trials [of being a U.S. Latino Muslim] is being patient with Muslims from Muslim countries who maintain a racist attitude toward other Muslims, especially toward converts."[67] This perception and the "newness" of the presence of the community are responsible

---

64. Conroy, *Betwixt & Between*, 53.

65. La Shure, "What is Liminality?," para. 24.

66. Conroy, 55.

67. Galván, "Thoughts among Latino Muslims," 14.

for the lack of programs and *da'wah* addressing the interests of the U.S. Latina/o Muslim community in most *masjids*. Galván reflects on this situation and explains that, "Unfortunately, some [who have been] raised [as] Muslims have negative stereotypes about Latinos," as they "think all Latinos are promiscuous and incapable of becoming a 'real' Muslim."[68] This condition amplifies the isolation U.S. Latina/o Muslims already confront from their own U.S. Latino community.

I argue that while this condition begins as a type of marginalization, as U.S. Latina/o Muslims begin to integrate into the larger Muslim community they find themselves in another liminal space. This is comparable with La Shure's personal narrative of liminality as "a Westerner living in Asia, suspended betwixt and between two cultures."[69] About his experience, he writes:

> When I first came to Korea, I was indeed marginal. I was marginalized by my ignorance of the Korean culture and language; in other words, I could not communicate with Koreans either culturally (that is, cultural differences prevented mutual understanding) or linguistically. As I became more familiar with both the culture and language, though, I moved into a liminal position. I am now part of Korean society to some extent, no longer fully liminal, but I will never be fully assimilated. I could return to my native land and be readily accepted there, but I doubt if I could ever fully accept my native land like I did before I left. I am betwixt and between.[70]

U.S. Latina/o Muslims share this experience of moving from marginality to liminality within the Muslim community, unlike their move from centre (normative) to liminality experienced within the U.S. Latina/o community. As La Shure did, they move forward with their process of developing a better understanding of Islam while identifying it as a way of life, which places them in the midst of the community, even if they are still seen with suspicion by some members of that community.

Thus, conversion to Islam places U.S. Latina/o Muslims in liminal spaces within two worlds, the U.S. Latina/o and the Muslim, while also putting them in-between these two worlds. But it is *because of* and *within* this condition of liminality, and within the cracks, that U.S. Latina/o Muslims start their process of identity re-construction. As La Shure

68. Galván, "FQAs about Latino Muslims," para. 18.

69. La Shure, para. 25.

70. Ibid., para. 26.

argues, "While in the liminal state, human beings are stripped of anything that might differentiate them from their fellow human beings – they are in between the social structure, temporarily fallen through the cracks, so to speak, and it is in these cracks, in the interstices of social structure, that they are most aware of themselves."[71] Thus, it is from this liminal space that U.S. Latina/o Muslims start challenging the normative presuppositions of both worlds, re-defining what it means to be a U.S. Latina/o and how Islam should be incorporated into that definition, while also proving that being a Latina/o should not be seen as contrary to being Muslim.

One of the first steps U.S. Latina/o Muslims take in order to address liminality is to create a community. Dispirited and feeling unwelcome, they are compelled to search for others "like them" in order to create connections, but as Gilberto, another U.S. Latino Muslim interviewed by Galván, explains, "One difficulty is that since there are a small number of us, there is a certain degree of aloneness compared to other communities, which have more members."[72] Galván summarizes these challenges by stating, "I feel alienated sometimes from the general Muslim population," and "because there aren't many Latino Muslims, I feel alienated sometimes from the general Latino population, too."[73] In this sense, U.S. Latina/o Muslims struggle to create their own spaces in the midst of isolation. Lewis Rambo, in talking about the effects of conversion, explains:

> In any case, conversion is precarious; it must be defended, nurtured, supported, affirmed. It needs community, confirmation, and concurrence. As converts develop spiritually, their understanding becomes more sophisticated and they review, reinterpret, and revalue their experience.[74]

It is within their liminality that U.S. Latina/o Muslims are forced to develop connections among themselves and for that matter to create a community. The creation of this community helps them address their isolation and as Rambo states, through them they can have a better understanding of their conversion.

Now, it is important to point out that when I talk about community in the case of U.S. Latina/o Muslims, I do not follow the traditional

---

71. Ibid., para. 15.
72. Galván, "Thoughts among Latino Muslims," 14.
73. Galván, "FQAs about Latino Muslims," para. 24.
74. Rambo, *Understanding*, 170.

conception of community. "The most common sociological definitions used today tend to focus on a community as an aggregate of people who share a common interest in a particular locality. Territorially based social organizations and social activity thus define a community."[75] The focus on place and territory is what is different in the case of how U.S. Latina/o Muslims build community. I am not arguing that they have not created social organizations within their physical location (e.g. their city), as I will explore in the next few pages, but that it was in a virtual space where community started to be built, outside of local organizations. For example, as mentioned in the previous chapter, the use of the Internet as a mode of communication has provided a space where people meet and share their experiences across towns, across the country, and across the world. This space becomes the site for the creation of community, which in many cases paved the way for the formation of many local U.S. Latina/o Muslim organizations. But, the actual creation of the U.S. Latina/o Muslim community is not restricted by place or formal structures since they have been able to mitigate the feelings of Otherness by coming together and understanding themselves as a group that, while not homogenous, still shares similar characteristics and purpose in the open spaces of the Internet.

This conception of community does not diminish the important role that the formation of local organizations has played in the creation of a U.S. Latina/o Muslim community. U.S. Latina/o Muslim organizations have formed in multiple cities across the United States, and their formation is a direct response to their liminality. At the same time, and aim of the formation of these organizations is also to create leaders within the community because, as Galván admits, "Latino Muslims do not have many role models." With strong and respected role models, the whole concept of Islam among U.S. Latina/os would likely become more acceptable.[76] These organizations bring U.S. Latina/o Muslims together to foster spiritual kinship and connection as well as social bonds and support. Some of these organizations offer a space for learning about Islam and the Qur'an in Spanish, and help create and propagate material about Islam in Spanish while others work to develop *da'wah* through the Internet.

In 1975, Alianza Islámica became the first U.S. Latina/o Muslim grassroots organization in the United States. This organization was

---

75. Bender, *Community and Social Change*, 5.

76. Galván, "Who are Latino Muslims?," 28.

founded in New York by a group of Puerto Rican converts, who were also involved in the social and political movements of the era—specifically civil rights and Puerto Rican nationalist struggles. In the midst of these struggles, they formed this organization in order to address the sense of isolation and marginalization that the Puerto Rican immigrant community was experiencing. Following the lead of other organizations, Alianza Islámica developed community programs to deal with gang violence, drug addiction prevention, and prostitution. At the same time, they were working on *da'wah* activities in the neighborhood and in some of the prisons. Through their activities within the community, activities such as weddings and prayers, among others, and through the inclusion of Puerto Rican music and food in those activities, Alianza was able to present itself as an intrinsic part of the local community, demonstrating the richness of the Puerto Rican culture and its connections to the Islamic culture.

Also in New York, Khadijah Rivera founded PIEDAD (Propagación Islámica para la Educación de Devoción Ala' el Divino). This organization "was formed to address issues affecting female reverts."[77] At the beginning PIEDAD developed strong missionary activities for Latinas in the United States, which included educational programs regarding marriage, the preparation of food, and how to deal with family members who had prejudices towards Islam. It functions as a volunteer-based organization, which in the past has worked with other Muslim groups like the International Islamic Federation of Student Organizations (IIFSO) in developing programs and seminars for the community. This organization, through the work of its chapters, continues to work with *da'wah* while also working with local Muslim communities in maintaining their effort to help new converts with everyday concerns. In order to truly affect the Latino community, they have been involved in translating literature on Islam into Spanish as well as in encouraging imams and other religious leaders to learn Spanish so that they can better serve all Muslim Americans.

The work that these and other local U.S. Latina/o Muslim organizations have done within their communities is invaluable. For example, the Los Angeles Latino Muslims Association (LALMA) "strives to provide spiritual support for the new Muslims by sharing a common language and culture," and recognizing "that all new Muslims must deal with personal habit and family concerns, LALMA assigns members to give

---

77. Rivera, "Empowering Latino Women," 37.

personal support to new Muslims."[78] But, these organizations do not have the reach that the Latino American Dawah Organization (LADO) has had. LADO "strives to educate Latinos and others about the legacy of Islam in Spain and Latin America and provide free information about Islam."[79] This grassroots organization was founded in 1997 in order to promote Islam among Latina/os in the United States and to create a network of support among them. Because of its use of the Internet, LADO has been able to create a Latina/o Muslim community that extends beyond the locality of a city. Through their website, they have been able to share conversion stories and *testimonios* from U.S. Latina/o Muslims in the form of an online newsletter. This newsletter is the place to read about community events across the United States and keep in touch with other individuals and organizations.

At the same time, LADO has been engaged in coordinating publications that give a public voice to the community. Juan Galván, executive director, was responsible for the publication of the first magazine issue dedicated to the presence of Latina/o Muslims in the United States, *Islamic Horizons* in July/August 2002. Later he became a guest editor of two editions of *Message International*, November/December 2004 and December 2005/January 2006 editions, also dedicated to the voices of the U.S. Latina/o Muslim community. This work and high profile coverage has turned LADO into the most popular missionary organization among Latina/o Muslims in the United States. They have been able to amplify the information about the community, which has in turn created a better understanding of U.S. Latina/o Muslims among non-Muslims.

These organizations may seem to have different specific functions, but in fact they share the same core mission.[80] In speaking about the importance and mission of these organizations, Galván states,

> Whereas some Muslim organizations serve many purposes, Latino Muslim organizations are primarily dawah organizations. Latino Muslim organizations agree about the importance of a full-fledged

78. Galván, "Latino Muslims," 36. It is important to acknowledge that the leaders of this organization declined my invitation to participate in this project and tried to bar others from participating, sending emails criticizing my intentions and character.

79. Zaid, "Latinos Eager for Islam," 30.

80. Some other organizations are the Chicago Association of Latino-American Muslims, California Latino Muslim Association, and Latino Muslims of the Bay Area. Members of these groups were interviewed for the construction of this book.

dawah effort to Latinos and agree that effective dawah to Latinos includes working with other Latino Muslims. Latino Muslim organizations also address the various needs of Latino Muslims by working to keep them as Muslims and to help them reach their full potential as Muslims. Latino Muslim organizations are a response to the various needs that are not being filled by the general Muslim community. Because Latino Muslims are an underrepresented segment of the Muslim community, the general Muslim population is not aware of many problems of interest to Latino Muslims.[81]

Yet the most important thing these connections promote is the re-conceptualization of who they are and the re-construction of their identities. I argue that the development of a community, which is in no way homogeneous, allows U.S. Latina/o Muslims the opportunity to address their liminality. In this community they are able to be themselves fully. They find a place, even if it is not always a physical one, where they can both live out their liminality and together with others engage in a process of dis-covering historical consciousness as they move to reconstruct their identities.

81. Galván, "The importance of Latino Muslim Organizations," para. 12.

3

Dis-covering: Reversion and Memory

I look forward to the day when folks can actually think of Latinos
as Muslims and be completely cool with it.[1]

THESE OPENING WORDS COME from Patricia, a particular U.S. Latina
Muslim from the Bay Area in California, but their sentiment is
shared by most U.S. Latina/o Muslims as they respond to their liminality and the desire not to feel like the "ugly-duckling" among U.S. Latina/
os. They themselves do not see any contradiction between their identities
and their newfound religion and often feel that their conversion—or better, reversion—to Islam in fact moves them closer to their *latinidad*. Yet
the popular perception is that after conversion U.S. Latina/o Muslims no
longer have legitimacy among the larger U.S. Latina/o community. Such
labeling and stereotyping makes them doubly liminal, doubly estranged
from the norm. For while ethnically they fit the oversimplified conception of what a U.S. Latina/o is, their conversion situates them without a
past that could support their actual "membership" within this community.
Normative historical narratives do not make any sense to U.S. Latina/o
Muslims because they do not recognize themselves in those narratives. At
the same time, because they feel somewhat separate from the larger U.S.
Muslim community, U.S. Latina/o Muslims once again are "in-between."
They see themselves as part of two different communities, the Latino
and the Muslim, and yet they are located in liminal spaces within both.
They are doubly "Other." So they search the past looking to retrieve a his-
torical consciousness and thus dis-cover a cultural memory. U.S. Latina/o
Muslims "remember" the past differently from the way it has become the
norm, in order to try and make sense of their culture and religion as non-

1. Interview with members of Latino Muslims of the Bay Area in Hayward, California
(July 30, 2006).

exclusive aspects, so that their new worldview has a connection to a past. This chapter explores how they do this.

Conversion implies a change in worldview not just a transformation of practices, or as Rebecca Sachs Norris acknowledges, "not just adopting a set of ideas but also converting to and from an embodied worldview and identity."[2] U.S. Latina/o Muslim converts, who for the most part were raised within a particular Christian worldview that has variously informed the development of most U.S. Latina/o identities, are consequently forced to challenge the normativity of the argument that U.S. Latina/o identities are strongly related to a Christian background. It becomes important for them to confront the historical construction of the stereotypical U.S. Latina/o identity, and dis-cover a new cultural memory that can serve as the core of their own process of re-construction of identities.[3] In other words, because U.S. Latina/os are mostly identified for their Catholic (or at least Christian) roots, U.S. Latina/o Muslims feel pressure to seek beyond that label and find an identity that puts together their ethnic (or national) characteristics and their religious experience in a way that makes sense to them.

As an outsider, it seems to me that the members of this community do not have a choice: they are forced to re-identify themselves. I am not simply alluding to the changes that conversion brings to every culturally distinct population, like changes in one's eating habits, one's name, or one's attire; I am talking about the much more essential process through which U.S. Latina/o Muslims have to re-invent themselves as people. This process of re-invention and re-construction of identity typically takes some time, but the nascent U.S. Latina/o Muslim communities are already forging the way, by rediscovering an earlier cultural memory and identity, one formed in their Muslim past of Spain.

---

2. Norris, "Converting to What?," 171.

3. In the process of revising my initial draft I shared it with the individuals I interview throughout the process of research. One of these individuals was concerned that he did not see this process as a re-construction but as an expansion of the identities. Since I view identities are fluid and never fixed (as a I will show later in this chapter), I do not see them expanding but always evolving and going through re-constructions, especially in the case of U.S. Latina/o Muslims that actually confront some of the established basis for the normative identities and deconstruct them.

IDENTITY

What is identity? Is it developed individually or through a group? How many identities can one have? Which one is the most important for a particular group: is it one's national, racial, ethnic, religious, cultural, or gender identity, or something else entirely? These questions have no single possible answer for these identities, whether self-created or imposed, are connected to labels and stereotypes fashioned in order to group, define, and shape individuals or communities for the sake of silencing or giving voice. As philosopher Kwame Anthony Appiah writes, "Once labels are applied to people, ideas about people who fit the label come to have social and psychological effects. In particular, these ideas shape the ways people conceive of themselves and their projects."[4] In this sense, labels are intrinsically tied not only to the way people see themselves but also to how they act. The presuppositions embedded within the labels influence their understanding of their history and social location. For example, when children are repeatedly told that they are lazy or dumb, they start believing it; the label becomes real in their minds and often in how they live their lives. Indeed, labels play "a role in shaping the way the agent makes decisions about how to conduct a life, in the process of the construction of one's identity."[5]

Identity derives from social contact and human interaction, and as a cultural phenomenon it is grounded in the interpretation of the past. Individual identities and collective identities are interrelated for they both constitute "a basic component of social life, of social order – like power and economic relations – which have indeed been continually interwoven with economic and power processes and relations."[6] As a social component of everyday life, identity has been understood for the most part in light of social systems of representations (labels). This implies that individuals and communities self-identify based on these labels and that these identifications may become fixed rather than evolving. But cultural theorist Stuart Hall suggests that "Identity is not as transparent or unproblematic as we think,"[7] and that, being linked to social and cultural aspects, it is always evolving. So Hall continues, "Perhaps instead of think-

---

4. Appiah, *The Ethics of Identity*, 66.

5. Ibid.

6. Eisenstadt, "The Construction of Collective Identities," 246.

7. Hall, "Cultural Identity and Diaspora," 110.

ing of identity as an already accomplished fact, which the new cultural practices then represent [labeling], we should think, instead, of identity as a 'production,' which is never complete, always in process, and always constituted within, not outside, representation."[8] This perspective challenges the perception that fixed and essentialized cultural and social representations are finished products. Identity is always evolving and transforming as a process grounded in historical consciousness, since identities are not formed in a vacuum or in an instant; they are based in particularities and are formed over time.

The construction of U.S. Latina/o identities is to my mind more akin to this understanding of identity as never finished, always fluid. The alternative, and more common labels or fixed identities, are part of a colonial enterprise, imposing stereotypes which blur the self, such that U.S. Latina/os, as colonial subjects, become Others within United States society. Colonial discourses have been responsible for fixing the identities of U.S. Latina/os first by erasing their history and then by imposing labels. U.S. Latina/o Muslims recognize the imposed stereotypes as inadequate, as unfitting or not fitting because they are colonial discourses. Instead, they engage in a process of identity re-construction, de-constructing the imposed identities and constructing alternative identities. These new identities are grounded in their capacity to become subjects by talking, self-identifying, and narrating their own history, not depending on other's perceptions. They become "historical subject[s] and agent[s] of an oppositional discourse."[9]

Such new identity constructions promote the re-interpretation and re-imagining of the past (a new historical consciousness), not for the sake of fixing historical representations, but to provide meaning and purpose to the process of ongoing transformation. Thus, identities are grounded in the cultural experience of the people, and for that matter "have histories" even if those histories "undergo constant transformation."[10] In this sense, identity constructions are not a matter of just looking at the past but of using historical consciousness in the interpretation of the past to search for meanings and identities. The process entails going beyond the traditional (colonial) stories in order to grasp what lies behind them, as it

8. Ibid.

9. Parry, "Problems in Current Theories," 44.

10. Hall, 112.

is here that "hidden" voices are located which help in the construction of identities within liminal spaces. U.S. Latina/o Muslims begin this process by confronting the social discourses that have fixed their identities and understanding their conversion in a historical perspective.

CONVERSION AND IDENTITY

Theologian V. Bailey Gillespie in his work *The Dynamics of Religious Conversion* states, "The question for those interested in identity is not whether religious conversion is valid in terms of theological truth but whether it is a part of an identity experience or can be contributory to it."[11] He goes on to answer the question in the affirmative by arguing that, "The religious conversion experience provides a turning point in the life of the young person or older adult and answers the questions raised when individuals face the problem of just what they are going to give their lives to or for."[12] Gillespie understands this relationship between conversion and identity in light of a theological paradigm, as the individual finds religious change and as that change affects the way she or he interprets the world. While I recognize the importance of this theological interpretation, my argument here goes beyond the theological interpretations of conversion as I look into the cultural and anthropological aspects that define religious conversion and how it affects the process of identity construction of the convert.

Religious experiences (or lack thereof) are an important part in the formation of identities because they are intrinsic to the individual's and the group's cultural worldview. Danièle Hervieu-Léger argues that, "The possibility that a group—or an individual—sees itself as part of a chain or lineage depends, to some extent at least, on mention of the past and memories that are consciously shared with and passed on to others."[13] Religion becomes one of those memories that are passed through generations and that help in the construction of a cultural worldview, an identity. In the case of U.S. Latina/os, the stereotype is that Christianity, specifically Catholicism, has served as the religious experience that facilitated the construction of normative understandings of U.S. Latina/o identities.

---

11. Gillespie, *The Dynamics of Religious Conversion*, 167.

12. Ibid.

13. Hervieu-Léger, *Religion as a Chain of Memory*, 123.

These understandings have been reproduced and have served as a way of defining this community. Hervieu-Léger argues:

> In the case of religious memory, the normativity of collective memory is reinforced by the fact of the group's defining itself, objectively and subjectively, as a *lineage* of belief. And so its formation and reproductiveness spring entirely from the efforts of memory feeding this self-definition. At the source of all religious belief . . . there is belief in the continuity of the lineage of believers. This continuity transcends history. It is affirmed and manifested in the essentially religious act of recalling a past which gives meaning to the present and contains the future.[14]

U.S. Latina/o identities have been defined through the preservation of the stereotype of a lineage of belief, grounded in the Spanish heritage of a Christian—and specifically Catholic—past creating what Hervieu-Léger calls an authorized memory that creates a lineage between the present and a particular past.[15] This authorized memory grounds the normative historical consciousness within the U.S. Latina/o consciousness. Thus, conversion to a new religious system affects and even interrupts this consciousness and the processes of identity construction.

Sometimes the affect of conversion on identity is larger than other changes "because religion is believed to be deeply rooted in the family connections, cultural traditions, ingrained customs, and ideologies."[16] The newfound religious system confronts the established system and for that matter confronts the identity of the individual and/or the group. For "minoritized" groups, the experiences of "hostility and prejudice from the wider society" serve to "sharpen the contours of identity," and thus a transformation of an essential aspect of that group's identity becomes critical.[17] In the case of U.S. Latina/o Muslims, their conversion and what it entails in regards to the normative historical consciousness becomes a moment of crisis of memory. Conversion becomes a moment of predicament in which the convert has to find a way to reconcile the identities formed before conversion with the new religious system that may or may not fit these identities.

14. Ibid., 125.

15. Ibid., 126.

16. Rambo, "Anthropology and the Study of Conversion," 212.

17. Gilliat-Ray, "Rediscovering Islam," 323.

U.S. Latina/o Muslims are forced to re-envision their culture as their new religious experiences do not fit the traditional understandings of *la-tinidad*. Juan Galván, from the perspective of a U.S. Latino Muslim, states, "We must strive to incorporate our culture by defining what Islam is and how our culture can adapt to it."[18] The initial stages of this process follow the theological interpretations Gillespie focuses on, as they are connected to their new religious practices and the commitment they make to the newfound religion. The converts see their changes as a way to re-organize their life in light of their new religious vision. But these changes are not limited to a theological interpretation because of the cultural connection to the religious practices. For example, we have seen that it general the U.S. Latino community perceives as strange for cultural and not just religious reasons the changes in the diet and clothes of their of their Muslim members.

Anthropologist Diane Austin-Broos explains conversion as a passage rather than as a complete break with the past. This conversion passage is a time of seeking out new meanings and connections. "Conversion is a type of passage that negotiates a place in the world. Conversion as passage is also quest, a quest to be at home in a world experienced as turbulent or constraining or, in some particular way, as wanting in value."[19] This passage does not imply a cultural breach, but a cultural dis-covery

---

18. Arroyo, "A Perspective from Chicago," para. 6. In conversations with Juan Galván over email in the past months, he reflected on this issue of culture and religion and specifically on some of his quotes regarding this issue. In an email message on June 7, 2009, he writes: "With regard to the quote that Latino Muslims "must strive to incorporate our culture by defining what Islam is and how our culture can adapt to it." That particular quote can be a bit confusing. It could easily be misinterpreted to mean that Latinos need to redefine Islam even though a basic Muslim belief is that Islam is perfect and doesn't need to be changed. The following quote is from an article I wrote, which expands on what I meant: "The Latino culture of today could become the Latino Muslim culture of tomorrow. Because Latino Muslims are a young community, clearly defining our Latino Muslim culture is difficult. Islam sets the framework and direction that the Latino Muslim culture takes. Taking up Islam means rejecting some old ways, accepting some new ways, and adapting when necessary." This does not seem to alter the point I am trying to put forward but on the other hand confirms it, as U.S. Latina/o Muslims are force to see beyond the normative understandings of identities and culture in order to construct a new one that fits them. The religious experience (Islam) serves as the basis for this re-construction and I argue that this experience, after conversion, opens the door for U.S. Latina/o Muslim converts to see beyond the established and normative historical consciousness.

19. Austin-Broos, "The Anthropology of Conversion," 2.

as the convert finds a way to make sense of the new religious experience and a new cultural identity. Conversion as a passage is continual and not static or fixed; it is always producing not just a change in social life, but also a change in meanings. Identity is then re-constructed to include this cultural dis-covery. As Karin van Nieuwkerk states, "Conversion is a multilayered, continuous process in which new identities and discourses are produced and reproduced."[20] Conversion provides a progress in the life of the convert from one state to another without a rupture because after all the new religious system can only be understood from the particular cultural location of the convert at the moment when conversion began. As Sachs Norris argues, "Given that cultural beliefs and practices shape experience, and that the meaning of religious language and ritual is grounded in embodied experience, converts initially understand the symbolism and language of their adopted religion through the filter of their original language and worldview."[21] Thus, converts opt for a new religious system not because it is totally different from the one they previously followed but because "it corresponds with ideas or wishes that have arisen within an existing psychological context."[22] Conversion is not just about a change in the religious aspect within identity; as a process, conversion has an effect on the individual's construction of the self, as a whole. Conversion provides them the opportunity of re-defining themselves since, as Rambo finds, "Central to the converting process is the convert's reconstruction of his or her biographical memory and deployment of a new system of attribution in various spheres of life."[23]

When U.S. Latina/os become Muslims they do not want to be seen as creating something new but rather to be locating their newfound religious experience in the context of their culture. They struggle to find an answer to the question: How does being a Muslim fit with being a U.S. Latina/o? This explains how the cultural passage can turn into a crisis of identity as they try to bridge their established worldview with the new one and as the convert begins to re-construct her/his identity. Gillespie speaks to this issue when he points out that, "What emerges in conversion could be a stable pattern, a context out of which life begins to be ordered," and that

20. van Nieuwkerk, "Gender and Conversion to Islam in the West," 10–11.
21. Norris, 171.
22. Ibid., 179.
23. Rambo, *Understanding*, 169.

"During this struggle identity is beginning to be formed, too."[24] While religious change brings some type of resolution to the initial crisis, the new religious experience leads to a crisis of identity that is addressed through cultural dis-covery rather than simple theological explanations. Such cultural dis-covery is best addressed in the context of group identities.

We saw in the previous chapter that as a consequence of conversion the convert finds him/herself in a liminal space because of the attitudes of those around her/him as they criticize or come to terms with that change. It is when the convert finds a community that she or he begins to re-construct her/his identity, re-envisioning culture together with the community. "This sense of belonging both supports the person's sense of identity and gives the person a network of people to serve and of which to be a part."[25] In this sense, the construction of the self should not be understood solely on the basis of a personal endeavor because "personal identity is related to the place of group think and group expectations."[26] Lewis R. Rambo affirms that, "Authentic conversion is a movement from mere personal conversion to a living out of conversion in the social world."[27] While conversion is based on an individual's decision for change, it also involves a social component and cannot be fully understood apart from the social connections and group identities developed as a consequence, hence my focus on community. As Gillespie finds, "identity and conversion often reorganize one around a new center of reference."[28] While the initial reorganization has to do with the convert's lifestyle, practices, and/or religious experiences, the ultimate reorganization that serves as the basis of identity construction is intrinsically related to the capacity of the individual to make sense of the decision in light of her/his culture. Thus, their participation within a group helps a person establish some of the parameters for identity construction.

I am not denying the importance of personal identity and the role that individual interests play in the process of conversion since it is clear that individuals are engaged in a personal search as part of their conversion. But this search develops into a crisis that needs to be addressed

24. Gillespie, 158.
25. Rambo, *Understanding*, 161.
26. Gillespie, 142.
27. Rambo, *Understanding*, 147.
28. Gillespie, 165.

in community and this community becomes a lens through which the convert sees the whole process of conversion and the way she or he constructs the conversion narrative.[29] As Rambo explains, one of the results of conversion is that the individual "may participate in a community of faith that connects him or her to both a rich past and an ordered and exciting present which generates a vision of the future that mobilizes energy and inspires confidence."[30] Stefano Allievi argues that, "Conversion, as entry into another culture and another religion, presupposes strong moments that symbolically sanction the conversion itself and reinforce its significance as a radical change and clean break with the past."[31] And yet U.S. Latina/o Muslims do not see conversion so much as a process of breaking with the past as an opportunity to look at it through a new historical consciousness and to dis-cover a cultural memory, which serves as the foundation for new identities.

REMEMBERING AND CULTURAL MEMORY

Historical narratives are constructed in order to give meaning to the present and the future through connections to the past. These connections are essential in the constructions of one's identities, and are always seen through a particular prism, not in a vacuum. Historical consciousness serves as that prism. As the Center for the Study of Historical Consciousness at the University of British Columbia explains on its website, "Historical consciousness can thus be defined as individual and collective understandings of the past, the cognitive and cultural factors which shape those understandings, as well as the relations of historical understandings to those of the present and the future." In this sense, historical consciousness is not limited to the past as it is formed out of the perspective of the present condition. Since after conversion the narratives of the past do not make sense through the lenses of the normative historical consciousness, U.S. Latina/o Muslims re-create their historical consciousness on the basis of their new socio-religious context, Islam. Through those new lenses, they re-read and re-interpret the historical narratives in order to acquire a connection to the past that actually fits with their present context, that

29. van Nieuwkerk, "Gender, Conversion, and Islam," 95–119.
30. Rambo, *Understanding*, 2.
31. Allievi, "The Shifting Significance," 124.

gives some cultural meaning to their conversion, and that serves as one of the foundations for the re-construction of their identities.

"Going back" implies an act of remembering and looking beyond the official narratives with a new historical consciousness. As U.S. Latina/o Muslims engage in this act they are able to dis-cover what is hidden within the narratives and thus challenge the knowledge that has come from these. This normative knowledge leaves many people's voices outside of its discourse just because they do not fit within the chosen narratives. The constructions of dominant identities are intrinsically related to these official stories and the knowledge they create.[32] On the other hand, by remembering and dis-covering the silences, individuals and groups that have been left out of the dominant identities engage in a subversive practice as they confront not only the narratives and knowledge created but also the identities formed out of these. This subversive activity can only be successful through the use of memory.

Memory is constantly linked to historical discourses, for the use of memory—the act of remembering—serves as the basis for constructing historical narratives. As Puerto Rican scholar Juan Flores reminds us, "*Memory* has been associated, since its earliest usages, with the act of inscribing, engraving, or, in a sense that carries over into our own electronic times, "re-cording" (*grabar*)."[33] In this sense, historical discourses serve as a representation/interpretation of memories. But within the process of re-construction of identities among U.S. Latina/o Muslims, memory acquires a more powerful positioning within historical discourses because "it may no longer be viewed merely as the raw material of history."[34] Using memory allows colonial subjects not only to recover what is lost in the narratives of history but also to challenge the very identities these narratives generate and legitimize. At the same time, the decline of the influence of these narratives of the past allows "for a proliferation of memory that talks back; not just recent memory, where it is most visible, but even distant forgotten memories that have returned to challenge history."[35]

32. These knowledges work as colonial discourses even if they were not created as such. Since they see themselves as "truth," they are not open to new possibilities and thus serve to silence those who do not fit.

33. Flores, "Broken English Memories," 338.

34. Dirlik, *Postmodernity's Histories*, 48.

35. Ibid., 48-49. This point becomes essential in the development of this book. While in this chapter I examine the use of cultural memories that are closer to the present,

Memory becomes a subversive activity as people dis-cover their histories previously suppressed by hegemonic histories, and recover "lost or suppressed identities."[36]

Using memory as subversive activity uncovers the fragmentation within historical narratives. While normative historical discourses are portrayed as linear and continuous, memory breaks that illusion, not in order to create a new continuous discourse but to reveal history as an ever-changing discourse. As Flores argues, since "the process of memory is open, without closure or conclusion: the struggle to (re)establish continuities and to tell the "whole" story only uncovers new breaks and new exclusions."[37] The decision turns out to be between remembering and forgetting. Both are processes of selecting what to remember and what to forget, but the act of remembering works against the metanarratives used to label and marginalize people and, for that matter, to break down the power they convey. Traditional historical discourses hide the voices of the colonized leaving them without a historical consciousness, but they also generate what Puerto Rican scholar Arcadio Díaz-Quiñones has identified as "broken memories."[38] *La memoria rota* (broken memory) is the product of the mutilation of a social consciousness. As Flores argues, "A peoples' memory and sense of collective continuity is broken not only by the abrupt, imposed course of historical events themselves, but by the exclusionary discourses that accompany and legitimate them."[39]

U.S. Latina/o Muslims, because of their liminality, suffer from "broken memories" and the subversive act of remembering allows them to re-establish those memories. Since this subversive activity is rooted in the cultural experience of the people, and not in an esoteric or academic interpretation of the past, U.S. Latina/o Muslims are not interested only in adding new raw material into the established narratives but in dis-covering new meanings and memories that transpire by exposing the discontinuities of the normative narratives. While those benefiting from colonial discourses may see the exposing of the discontinuities as "a threat to cultural survival and inclusion," such exposure allows the colonial subject to

---

U.S. Latina/o Muslims draw on "distant forgotten memories" in their process of identity construction.

36. Ibid., 48.

37. Flores, 338.

38. Díaz-Quiñones, *La Memoria Rota*, 1993.

39. Flores, 340.

"critically examine prevailing continuities and imagine and create new ones."[40] Consequently, these discontinuities exposed through the act of remembering "manifest themselves in lived experience and expression."[41] For U.S. Latina/o Muslims the practice of Islam, beyond the centrality of its spiritual character, is understood as a lived experience that has a cultural character grounded in a historical past that should be remembered. Thus, the remembered past becomes part of the lived experience.

This re-conceptualization of the past as part of the lived experience is grounded in the understanding that "history is constructed partially from the accounts of witnesses and partially from primary documents that reveal the memories of those involved in the events."[42] In essence, history should not be seen as a simple recollection of facts from the past, but as "a reconstruction of culturally relative "facts" that is always influenced by particular worldviews."[43] Cultural location adds to historical discourses not only a sense of specificity but also a meaning grounded in the experience of a particular community in the same way that Stuart Hall states that one cannot understand identity outside of its cultural location. Historical interpretation thus does not come from a one-dimensional impetus for understanding the past in a vacuum but from the necessity of locating oneself within the present and the future. In this way, the subversive activity of remembering is a cultural activity, which I refer to here as cultural memory.

Cultural memory can be seen as both an individual and a collective experience.[44] The use of cultural memory offers people more than the opportunity to recall the past in order to find continuity. For example, as Jan Assmann states, there are other types of memory, like communicative memory, which is used "to describe the social aspect of individual memory."[45] On the other hand, bonding (and collective) memory is used to illustrate Nietzsche's understanding "that people need a memory in order to be able to form bonds."[46] The English-language words *re-membering*

---

40. Ibid., 342.

41. Ibid., 347.

42. Rodríguez and Fortier, *Cultural Memory*, 11.

43. Ibid.

44. Bal, "Introduction," vii.

45. Assmann, *Religion and Cultural Memory*, 3.

46. Ibid., 5.

and *re-collecting* express with particular clarity this "bonding nature of memory," which is essential within the process of creating identity. They evoke the idea of putting "members" back together (re-membering and dis-membering) and "re-collecting" things that have been dispersed."[47] This "coming together" by "putting together" exemplifies the way communities see the past as a source for connection among their members. U.S. Latina/o Muslim, as subjects in search of identities, through a process of dis-covery, re(member) and re(collect), not as an individual enterprise, but as a communal and socially situated activity. But bonding memories can limit the understandings we have about the past and ourselves and for that reason we need to go beyond simply gathering bonding memories and also add the cultural perspective. Through cultural memory, the memories of the past are not limited to organized traditions and history, but include those stories that are not narrated within the official history, "the noninstrumentalizable, heretical, subversive, and disowned."[48] Cultural memory generates knowledge that is beyond traditional western knowledge, and through the use of a re-created historical consciousness, U.S. Latina/o Muslims access this type of memory—a vital task since the normative knowledge has covered, erased, and silenced it.[49]

Thus, U.S. Latina/o Muslims will look to the past for a representation and interpretation of the "facts" and memories from their particular location, using lenses that look beyond the traditional history. In this sense, "memory becomes important as a survival mechanism when it becomes part of artistic, emotionally laden ways of forming group identity and meanings."[50] This dis-covery of a cultural memory, in light of the community's historical consciousness, brings forward hybrid identities that challenge the essentialized versions of identity established by colonial discourses. Along with Jeanette Rodríguez and Ted Fortier, I understand cultural memory as "rooted in actual events and in the surrounding and resulting alignment of images, symbols, and affectivities that turn out to

---

47. Ibid., 11.

48. Ibid., 27.

49. It is important to establish at this point that I recognize that those cultural memories may have been covered for reasons that are not related to U.S. Latina/o Muslims, but as the knowledge have been constructed as the "truth" it does not allows for the discovery of these memories. In this case, the cultural memories to be dis-covered are based on the importance of a Muslim Spain.

50. Rodríguez and Fortier, 10.

be even more persuasive than facts."[51] The use of cultural memory brings together the re-interpretation of the past with the lived experience of the people allowing U.S. Latina/o Muslims to construct hybrid identities different from those imposed through the process of stereotyping. The re-interpretation begins with the personal stories in order to move to the more general stories. This means that U.S. Latina/o Muslims after conversion re-create their historical consciousness that provides the basis for the re-interpretation of the past beginning with their own personal narratives and moving to the dis-covery of cultural memories that affect the re-construction of identities for the group.

RE-INTERPRETING PERSONAL STORIES

The construction or re-construction of identity after religious conversion takes many forms. Elena, from Los Angeles, believes that besides the changes in clothing and diet, she does not see any changes in the way she looks at her culture. She argues that her new religion does not influence her ethnic identity and it does not change the way she feels about her Mexican nationality.[52] But Elena's story is not typical: most U.S. Latina/o Muslims see conversion as an opportunity to re-invent themselves, to search for a new identity. Erik, a U.S. Latino Muslim from the Bay Area, finds that "becoming Muslim empowered [his] identity as being Latino."[53] Conversion became a process through which he could start looking at himself in a different way as he became more aware about the meaning of his own ethnicity. He "feel[s] like [he is] more Latino now than [he] was when [he] wasn't Muslim."[54] Through the adoption of a new religion, Erik not only re-directs his spiritual life but also re-focuses on the construction of his identity.

José, also from the Bay Area, goes even further: he says conversion allowed him to see *latinidad* beyond the traditional categories of color, language, or nationality because "becoming" a Latino was not a choice while the religious conversion was. In his analysis, his decision for Islam made religion not an intrinsic aspect of the culture but an aspect sepa-

51. Ibid.,11.

52. Interview with a group of U.S. Latina/os in Los Angeles (July 28, 2006).

53. Interview with members of Latino Muslims of the Bay Area in Hayward, California (July 30, 2006).

54. Ibid.

rated from culture. At the same time, José was clear to mention that he doesn't "think Islam makes [him] feel less Latino," but on the contrary the newfound religion "does empower" who he is.[55] Edgar, a U.S. Latino Muslim from Los Angeles, argues that after conversion he grew stronger in his ethnicity because he started studying his own Mexican American culture at the same time he continued to study Islam. Before conversion, "culture really wasn't an interest to [him]," since he just considered himself Mexican, but now he wants "to study a little bit more in detail."[56] These U.S. Latino Muslims acknowledge the importance of conversion in their process of identity re-construction as they are able to move beyond the spiritual aspects of their decision into a deeper understanding of their transformation. In other words, converts see their religious experience of conversion as a process that informs the re-defining of their whole identity, not just their religious identity.

U.S. Latina/o Muslims do not simply re-focus their spirituality by transforming their daily activities; they also develop a re-interpretation of their personal narrative. This part of the process of identity construction is essential because it seeks to provide a narrative through which the religious transformation becomes an integral part of life's story and not just an event that doesn't make any sense. Thus, as the conversion narratives in the first chapter prove, individuals begin with a re-interpretation of their personal narratives and then move to re-construct the historical narratives that serve as the norm. While "a common observation is that Islam appeals because it gives the convert the greatest possible contrast with the culture he or she comes from,"[57] U.S. Latina/o Muslims seek to find the connections between their culture and the newfound religion, and thus conversion is not seen as a way of turning away from their culture.

For most, as Erik and José show, the crisis that arises as a result of conversion creates the possibility of re-engaging their personal narrative and re-interpreting it in light of their transformation, and many find that conversion allows them to re-think their ethnicity. Individuals look at their pasts and begin to challenge the official history. They start to look at history as a source of empowerment because in the narratives of the past they find sources for the re-construction of a historical conscious-

---

55. Ibid.

56. Interview with a group of U.S. Latina/os in Los Angeles (July 28, 2006).

57. van Nieuwkerk, "Gender and Conversion to Islam in the West," 6–7.

ness. These narratives are not typically the ones that dominate historical discourses but those that have been silenced. The yearning for this discovery wasn't there before because we take for granted the stories we are told and the silences. Yet when a crisis comes we start looking beyond these stories and start filling up the silences. In this case, the crisis comes as U.S. Latina/o Muslims experience a condition of liminality within both the U.S. Latino community and the larger Muslim community. This crisis is what opens the door to a re-interpretation of the past in order to find a narrative that fits.

Patricia wasn't aware of her family history before she converted to Islam, but dis-covered that through Islam she was compelled to move beyond the narratives she was told. She states, "I think coming to Islam, for me, it kind of gave me the yearning for this history."[58] Finding, among other things, that there are Native American roots within her family allowed her to see her background in a larger context, which in itself opened the door to do more searching, beyond her individual history. Consequently, she began looking into the importance of Spain in the construction of who she is as a U.S. Latina.[59] In the same way, Erik felt empowered by embracing Islam not just for what it did to his spiritual life but because he found that "the facts that we're connected to Mexico and Spain" made sense.[60] As Félix concludes, reflecting on this conversation, "now [they] have the moral responsibility to find about [their] roots, [their] history, all of [their] sides."[61] By finding out more about their *latinidad*, they become better equipped to speak to their children and others about the meaning of their culture.

Rafael pushes the discussion even further by connecting this responsibility to Islamic law. He states, "I feel much more empowered [now] that I [am] more informed about myself and about the Latino culture."[62] For him, "one of the five Muslim maxims" speaks to the importance that

58. Interview with members of Latino Muslims of the Bay Area in Hayward, California (July 30, 2006).

59. The dis-covery of Spain as central aspect of their historical consciousness is essential in their process of re-construction of identity. In the next section, I focused on this aspect.

60. Interview with members of Latino Muslims of the Bay Area in Hayward, California (July 30, 2006).

61. Ibid.

62. Ibid.

"customs and traditions carry."[63] Rafael's reflection speaks to the connection U.S. Latina/o Muslims constantly seek between their culture and the newfound religion in order to challenge the critiques regarding their lack of *latinidad*. For Rafael, it is important to understand that "Latino culture and Islamic culture are very intertwined," as it is exemplified in the similarities of "language, architecture, sayings and customs."[64] María finds that except for wearing *hijab*, things that involve a Muslim and his life are not that different from U.S. Latinos.[65] For her, focusing on the resemblance becomes the means she uses to talk about her experience in Islam and to explain how U.S. Latina/os do not lose their *latinidad* in the transition after their conversion. She explains:

> And I tend to assume that's simply because we have African obviously in us. I met a group of Moroccans and they were like so many Puerto Ricans. I told them: "You guys are just like us, there are hardly any differences [between us] except the language, whatever, and maybe the religion." But in terms of the men, the way they protect and lead the family, and the women, *sencilla*, *humilde*, you know, caring, take care of the family--those roles are very much a part of a Muslim's life. And so you will find a bunch of Latinos who come to Islam because it's like a transition. It wasn't a big transition for me to become a Muslim; it was a life I was leading already because I am a *Boricua* and my family is this way.[66]

Finding the similarities between these cultures is essential in the process of reconstructing identity as it allows the individuals to establish connections. Thus the conversion process doesn't become a path of uncertainty, but as María mentions, a transition. In this transition, most U.S. Latina/o Muslims experience what Félix sees as "a rebirth of our culture."[67] Hence, as much as conversion to Islam encourages U.S. Latina/os to dis-cover their particular (Moorish) roots and history, many also see it as an opportunity to transform the whole culture.

Such transformations of the culture begin individually. One changes one's life for the better and offers it as an example of what the culture may

63. Ibid.

64. Ibid.

65. Interview with María in New York City (July 23, 2006).

66. Ibid.

67. Interview with members of Latino Muslims of the Bay Area in Hayward, California (July 30, 2006).

be. For U.S. Latina/o Muslims, the struggle to become recognized among the larger U.S. Latino community makes this individual process harder and the communal experience among the members of this group becomes an important aspect in the transformation. Thus, the communal activity and the solidarity found in the U.S. Latino Muslim organizations allows for the possibility of identity construction beyond the simple transformation of the spiritual aspects of life. It allows for re-encountering the culture. In community, these Muslims not only feel part of something but also find a secure place to re-invent themselves. Omar finds that his "getting together with the brothers" provides a site of learning, not only about Islam but also about himself.[68] In this setting the personal histories are put together and group identities are developed. As in the case of individual U.S. Latina/o Muslim identities, these group identities are also based on the re-creation of a historical consciousness. As I mentioned before, the group engages in the re-construction of the past by challenging the official history and "remembering" those cultural memories that have been hidden by that history. U.S. Latina/o Muslims "go back" or revert and remember the history about a Muslim Spain, which have been covered by the normative historical narratives.

REVERSION: GOING BACK

Historian Alberto Hernández explains that U.S. Latina/os "have looked back upon their Iberian cultural and family heritage with an ambivalence not easily understood by persons of Anglo-European or Germanic ancestry."[69] This ambivalence arises from the connection that the Iberian heritage has with "the trappings of Spanish conquest and colonial exploitation."[70] Colonization and conquest, thus, have become the particular terms that describe the history of Spain's relationship to Latin America. On the other hand, U.S. Latina/o Muslims who do not dispute this colonial narrative look to Spain in a different way because they in clude Spain's history prior to colonization and conquest. They are interested in re-constructing the traditional and normative narratives to discover the cultural memories about Islam that have been hidden in order to underscore the Catholic tradition that lay behind the course of the col-

---

68. Ibid.

69. Hernández, "Hispanic Cultural Identity," 41.

70. Ibid.

onization and conquest of the Americas. At the same time, "Spain and its history was marginalized by intellectuals and nationalists touting the racialized nineteenth-century discourses of Western European civilization."[71] The contact and exchange between three cultures—Muslim, Jewish, and Christian—generated a mixed society, a hybrid reality, which placed Spain outside of the paradigm European modernity created. Describing this situation, Hernández states that, "when the intellectual and literary canon of European civilization was constructed by nineteenth-and early twentieth-century Euro-American intellectuals, Spain was marginalized for not being "white" enough and still too mired in a latent "medievalism" to have benefitted from the ideals and objectives of the Enlightenment."[72]

U.S. Latina/o Muslims re-interpret the history of Spain beyond its relation to Latin America, arguing that the period of three cultures, especially due to the dominance of Islam, not only does not reduce Spanish history but on the contrary makes it rich. The focus on the richness of this forgotten history does not simply allow for the re-construction of historical consciousness through the dis-covery of cultural memories, but also leads U.S. Latina/o Muslims to create a cultural identity that has at its core this covered part of history. Thus, after conversion, U.S. Latina/o Muslims go through a series of steps that lead to that creation of identity. They transform their personal lives and they "go back" and re-member (put together) those silenced features of the past in order to transform normative historical consciousness and help explain how their conversion actually fits their *latinidad*. Dis-covering the cultural memories of the Islamic tradition within the Spanish history and culture, U.S. Latina/o Muslims understand their conversion as a process of "going back" to the roots of what it means to be a Latina/o. For this reason, most U.S. Latina/o Muslims refer to their process of conversion as a process of reversion, a process of returning. U.S. Latino Muslim Yahya 'Abu Ayah' López explains this process:

> When we said that we "reverted" back to Islam, we therefore were, in effect, saying that we had returned, migrated back, or come home to our original condition from which we had been tragically separated in years past. After voluntarily returning to that primordial form, we then joyfully "embraced" it. We had realized, via our

71. Ibid., 44.
72. Ibid.

93

cognitive evaluation, its true worth and held it tightly within our arms, not wanting to let it go again.[73]

Reversion thus represents not stepping away from their cultural and historical memory but recovering their past and the "forgotten" (dis-membered) heritage of a Muslim Spain. This "going back" tends for the most part to romanticize Moorish culture and history. As community leader Edmund A. Arroyo explains, "The Latino Muslim conversion can often be traced to this rediscovery of their ancestral roots."[74] This is a way of looking at the past in order to dis-cover a "new" cultural memory, hidden behind the colonial discourses. Thus, "reversion" explains both the religious "going back" to Islam and the "going back" to the Muslim roots in the Latino cultural memory.

The concept of reversion allows us to see beyond the natural changes U.S. Latina/o Muslims go through and understand how they go beyond describing their conversion. With this concept and understanding of "going back," they address the criticism of and challenge to their *latinidad* posed by other members of the U.S. Latina/o community. U.S. Latina/o Muslims typically find many similarities between Islam and Latino culture, rather than seeing these two cultures as opposites as do many outside this community. Establishing these connections is only the first step in the process of building an identity founded in cultural memories that are in need of dis-covery, and a historical consciousness developed out of these dis-coveries. When asked about how she reconciles her reversion with the challenges to her Latina identity, María clearly establishes that reversion has actually cemented her understanding of her *latinidad*:

> Actually, I feel it has reinforced my identity because in my perspective I am actually going back to my roots. I think people who are Christian, who are Catholic, have gone away from their Latino roots because we have our roots in Spain. We have our roots in the Moors. Our language contains Arabic words. Our morality, our chivalry, the men, their protection, how they are with their women, with their families, that comes from the Arabs, from the Moors. So, I think I am reinforced. I think I am in an uphill battle because some people's perspectives are now the norm and that is

73. López, "What's in a Word," para. 8.

74. Arroyo, para. 3.

what I am dealing with. But, I do not feel displaced or like I am going against my Latino roots.[75]

Many U.S. Latina/o Muslims share this same perspective and look at this history as the basis of their new identity. As María, some will take personal issue with the challenges and push back by challenging the Christian privilege within history and arguing that it is in the Moorish tradition that one can find the actual roots of *latinidad*. This discussion regarding the role Muslim, and even Jewish, traditions plays within the history of Spain has always been a topic of dispute among historians and philologists. While I will not thoroughly analyze the entire dispute nor manage to do justice to its complexity, even examining just a few aspects of it helps us to understand why this "going back" makes sense for U.S. Latina/o Muslims' identity construction.

A MUSLIM SPAIN

"The first Muslims had arrived in the Iberian Peninsula in 711; the mass expulsion of all Muslims was decreed and carried out in the period 1609–14, nine centuries later."[76] Spanish historiography is filled with multiple interpretations of this period and the importance of the Muslim presence in the country, but no matter one's perspective, the meaning of this period tends to define the way the Spanish civilization is understood. As philologist James T. Monroe finds, "Mention of the Arabs and their role in the formation of Spanish culture has for many centuries elicited a widely varying response among Spanish scholars, ranging from outright hostility on the one hand, to gullible and uncritical acceptance of the most extravagant hypotheses concerning Arab 'influences' on the other."[77] Some scholars focus their analysis on the events of 1492 and the society they created, many times dismissing the effects of what Spanish philologist Américo Castro refers to as the intermingling of three castes of believers.[78] By highlighting the triumph of Catholicism, the history of the Spain of three cultures is left out and thus forgotten. This approach has the effect of trying to locate Spanish civilization within the European paradigm. On the other hand, scholars like Castro assess that the meaning of Spanish

75. Interview with María in New York City (July 23, 2006).

76. Harvey, *Muslims in Spain*, 1.

77. Monroe, "The Hispanic-Arabic World," 69.

78. See Castro, *The Spaniards*.

civilization should be understood "as a single cultural, social, and historical unit," as demonstrated by "the intimate, and often intricate, interrela-
tionship of Christianity, Islam and Judaism in the history of Spain."[79] They
continue that the history of Spain "must be viewed as a special historical
phenomenon to which the historical categories of other European nations
are not applicable."[80] Américo Castro explains that, "the history of Spanish
culture cannot be undertaken from a point of view virtually foreign to it,
because then we would be talking about something that does not exist
and we would fail to perceive the essence of its values."[81]

The presence and interaction of three cultures in Spain created
a different historical panorama there from the rest of Europe, and it is
in this interaction that the founding principles of Spanish identity are
found. Silencing some of the voices (typically the Muslim and the Jewish)
involved in this development of identity leads to the construction of a
false identity. Castro makes the case that, "Insufficient observation and
interpretation have been devoted to certain Spanish ways of living and
speaking which have no meaning when removed from their Islamic frame
of reference."[82] In his *Origen, ser y existir de lo españoles*, Castro even titles
the first chapter "El Al-Andalus y los orígenes de la españolidad," signal-
ing that the phase of Islamic presence is at the core of the construction
of Spanish identity.[83] With the work of Américo Castro establishing the
importance of these interrelationships, "one of the most famous polemics
in the history of Hispanic studies was launched."[84] An analysis of Castro's
perspective in this polemic facilitates the understanding of U.S. Latina/o
Muslims' argument for dis-covering cultural memories through the re-
construction of historical consciousness.

Américo Castro did not see Spanish civilization, or its history, as
something fixed or static, but as something "dinámica, complicada y fe-

---

79. Holmes, "Review," 1031.

80. Ibid.

81. Castro, "The Meaning of Spanish Civilization," 24. Philologist Guillermo Araya
Goubet finds that, "It was when Américo Castro found himself in disagreement with the
Europeanizing view of Spain that he began the long process of seeking out a satisfactory
way to make the history of his people understandable in his own eyes." [Araya Goubet,
"The Evolution of Castro's Theories," 50.]

82. Castro, *The Spaniards*, 272.

83. See Castro, *Origen, ser y existir de lo españoles*.

84. López-Baralt, "The Legacy of Islam in Spanish Literature," 518.

cunda" (dynamic, complicated and fertile).[85] Manuel Durán argues that with this vision of history Castro confronted three different static interpretations of the history of Spain: 1) that of an eternal Spain in which the characteristics of the Spanish have been set and fixed in pre-history, 2) that of an exclusive Christian reality of medieval Spain, which dismisses the interaction between the other religions, and 3) an interpretation one tied to the Golden era, which hides anxieties and persecutions, insecurities and frustrations.[86] In this sense, Spanish history is not simple or defined by one tradition or institution, but by the interaction between three religions and cultures. "This coexistence of different religious groups in medieval Spain is often described by the particular term *convivencia*"[87]—for Castro "a living-togetherness in the Christian kingdoms from the tenth to the end of the fifteenth century of people of three castes: Christian, Jewish, and Mudejar."[88] In the understanding of this *convivencia* lies the meaning of the period and "the key problem of authentically Spanish history."[89]

The problem is that using the term *convivencia* may give the false impression that the period of three cultures in Spain can be simply described as a period of harmony without controversy or disagreements. In trying to break with such a simplistic interpretation, religious historian Lucy K. Pick finds that this term "describes a cultural situation in which potential cooperation and interdependence in economic, social, cultural, and intellectual spheres coexist with continual threat of conflict and violence."[90] But amid these different perspectives, some scholars underscore, as Américo Castro did, that even within the tensions of the period there was a culture of tolerance among the various groups. It is this culture of tolerance that María Rosa Meocal stressed as being the truer definition of this era, not simply politically but also culturally.[91] This culture helps establish the basis of the interaction between the different groups, and helps create others. As Puerto Rican philologist Luce López-Baralt argues, "The coexistence of the Moors and the Christians was intense and widespread, and

85. Durán, "Américo Castro y la Identidad de los Españoles," 88.

86. Ibid., 88-89. (My translation)

87. Pick, *Conflict and Coexistence*, 1.

88. Castro, *The Spaniards*, 584.

89. Ibid., 59.

90. Pick, 1. Also see Fletcher, *Moorish Spain*. Fletcher dedicates a whole chapter to the issue of *convivencia*, describing the discriminations and conflicts of this time.

91. See Menocal, *The Ornament of the World*.

gave rise to such hybrid groups as the Mudejars (Muslims living among Christians) and the Mozarabs (Islamised Christians)."[92] We can minimize but not deny the intricacies of the relationships between these groups and the reality of the cultural effects on that history and society. For Castro, especially those cultural aspects connected to Islamic roots become the features that serve to explain the creation of Spain, even in the midst of a complex history.

This complex history is explained by the fact that, "Spain is the only European country that was simultaneously Occidental and Oriental in the first centuries of its formation as a nation, and it is impossible to imagine that this unique historical situation was without consequences."[93] The effect of Islamic culture can be seen in multiple facets of Spanish life. For example, even in the contested medieval era in Spain, "it was the Arabs who took al-Andalus to scientific and artistic heights unattained by any other country in Europe at this period."[94] In this sense, Islamic culture affected the construction of identity on multiple levels and a look through the literature of the era shows that its prominent role is clear. From *El Poema del Mio Cid* and *Don Quijote* to *El Libro del Buen Amor*, the presence of Islamic culture is ubiquitous. For example, in *El Poema del Mio Cid*, "Spain's foremost epic poem," the author "calls the hero by an Arabic name (*Mío Cid* meaning 'my lord')."[95] The poets and novelists of the time were quite aware of the important role Islamic traditions play in the construction of Spanish culture, and their work represents that interaction between groups. Further, López-Baralt finds that not only Spanish literature is indebted to Islam, but also Spanish mysticism, as in the case of St. John of the Cross.[96] This confirms Américo Castro's argument about how much even the creation of Spanish religion, which "is based on a Catholicism very different from that of Rome and France," needs to be understood in light of "the 900 years of Christianity-Islamic-Jewish interaction."[97]

---

92. López-Baralt, 518.

93. Ibid., 505.

94. Ibid., 515.

95. Ibid., 526.

96. Ibid., 528–32.

97. Castro, *The Structure of Spanish History*, 122.

Clearly the importance of Islamic traditions cannot be hidden. They served as an essential part of the creation of a hybrid culture and affected the way of life in Spain.[98] At the same time, immigrant Muslim communities refer to this era as emblematic. Hisham Aidi states:

> For many of the minority convert communities and the diaspora Muslim communities, Islamic Spain has emerged as an anchor for their identity. Moorish Spain was a place where Islam was in and of the West, and inhabited a Golden Age before the rise of genocidal, imperial West, a historical moment that disenchanted Westerners can share with Muslims.[99]

In this sense, the dis-covery of the central role that Islamic traditions had in the creation of the Spanish civilization offers an opportunity to re-construct a historical consciousness and build an identity upon a dis-covered cultural memory.

BUILDING ON THE PAST

U.S. Latina/o Muslims focus their attention on the dis-covery of these cultural intricacies in order to demonstrate the central role Islam plays in their historical consciousness and for that matter in the construction of their identities. In this regard, Juan Galván states that, "Latinos today are still influenced by Islamic Spain" and that, "for example, thousands of Spanish words are derived from Arabic."[100] Some of these words like *ojalá*, which comes from the Arabic *Insha'Allah* (God willing) and words that begin with *al* like *almohada*, which comes from *almuhádda* (pillow), pervade the Spanish language, and show the connection. Raheel Rojas, a U.S. Latino Muslim writing in *The Latino Muslim Voice*, focusing on this perspective about Muslim Spain being at the core of U.S. Latina/o identity, makes a plea to U.S. Latina/o Muslims who doubt their *latinidad*:

---

98. "To put it differently, the Spanish Empire, with all its extraordinary achievements, would not have been possible as we know it, had not the Spanish people learned how to be religious imperialists from their Muslim enemies. And so, in reading Castro's works we come to the inevitable conclusion that medieval, as well as many aspects of modern Spain, cannot be understood properly if they are separated from the Islamic elements and context that formed so integral a part of them." [Monroe, "The Hispanic-Arabic World," 75-76.]

99. Aidi, "Let Us Be Moors," para. 43.

100. Galván, "Who are Latino Muslims?," 28.

> What can be more Latino that being Muslim? Spain was predomi-
> nantly Muslim for 800 years. The shining light of Islam belonged to
> people who spoke Spanish, mashallah. Europeans came to Spain to
> learn sciences. Spain brought the renaissance of Christian Europe.
> Islam spread in Spain through the reversion of the indigenous
> people not mass immigration of Moors as they have you believe.[101]

In this sense, Muslim Spain becomes the center in the process of re-
construction of identity. Kenny Yusuf Rodríguez, a Dominican Muslim,
who argues that most of the Latina/os that criticize Islam do so because
they may have "forgotten that Islamic and Spanish cultures were once
closely knit," goes even further to link Islam in Spain and Latin America
as he stresses the Islamic influences not only in language, but also in
architecture.[102]

In the same way, Ramón Omar Abduraheem Ocasio establishes,
"We are reclaiming our history after a 500 year hiatus" because "Catholics
never successfully stripped the Moors of their identity," and thus "We are
the cultural descendents of the Moors."[103] These types of argument increase the visibility of these stories from the past in order to establish the
importance of Islamic culture as part of the basis for U.S. Latina/o culture.
While some, like María, offer a critique of Catholicism as dominant, most
U.S. Latina/o Muslims highlight Islamic culture in Spain as being not oppressive and colonizing but inclusive and tolerant. This idea of Spanish
civilization is what U.S. Latina/o Muslims want to dis-cover: that Islamic
culture is a culture of tolerance and that it is part of the core of Spanish
identity and civilization. It has been hidden by the preponderance of the
Spanish narratives that only emphasize the "Occidental" aspects of its history, thus stressing the Catholic perspectives. While in dis-covering the
hidden stories and re-constructing the narratives U.S. Latina/o Muslims
seem to take a romantic approach to Islamic culture at the same time they
underscore that the Spanish Catholic history of colonization cannot be
understood without a full comprehension of the interactions between the
three cultures.[104]

101. Rojas, "In Between Religions," para. 9.

102. Rodríguez, "Latino Muslims," 40–41.

103. Aidi, "Olé to Allah," 26.

104. Américo Castro argues that Spanish attitudes towards indigenous populations
and African enslaves came as a direct result of their attitudes towards Muslims and Jewish
in Spain who were used as servants. At the same time, Castro also recognizes the Islamic

Their attitude resembles that of Spanish Muslims and Moriscos (Muslims or descendants who converted or were forced to convert), who after 1492 resisted the imposition by those (Christians) in power of a national myth that left Al-Andalus and Islamic tradition out of the picture, a myth "that veiled its divisive regionalism and sacralized its origin in the Crusades of the Reconquest."[105] Historian Mary Elizabeth Perry maintains that as part of the challenge to that national myth, Muslims "claimed their own myths of the past," that allowed them "to resist oppression and reclaim their position of honor and power."[106] The confrontation of these two myths created a debate regarding the legacies that served in the construction of Spanish identity, which resulted in the evolution of what Perry calls contested identities, each based on a different myth. The struggle between these contested identities forced those in power both to expel Muslims and Jews from Spain and to reinforce the myth of a Catholic, Occidental Spain, leaving the "Other" (Muslims and Jews) outside of the myth. U.S. Latina/os, who after conversion to Islam no longer recognize themselves in the official history, reclaim that Islamic myth, and create a space of contested identities among U.S. Latina/os.[107] In the process of reconstructing their identity, they realize that their hybrid identities are complicated even further if they can dis-cover the Islamic tradition embedded within *latinidad*.

This process of re-construction is comparable to that undertaken by some U.S. African American Muslims who through their own *da'wah* search deeper into the past in order to make sense of their social condition and to create new identities. This message "raised the consciousness of [U.S.] African Americans about their history, including the fact that many of them were descendants of Muslims who had been forcibly converted to Christianity."[108] At the same time, Islamist Sherman A. Jackson argues that "rather than any African connection," other factors "paved the

style in the construction of churches (columns), which underscore the connection to Islamic culture. [Castro, *Iberoamérica*, 9-12.]

105. Perry, *The Handless Maiden*, 37.

106. Ibid.

107. This interest in dis-covering this history is present the large amount of articles on the topic within newsletters dedicated to U.S. Latina/o Muslims. For example see Sánchez, "Islamic Resurgence in Spain and Beyond," no pages, and Santos García, "Musulmanes en la Península Ibérica," no pages, among others.

108. Haddad, "The Quest for Peace in Submission," 21.

way for Blackamericans to establish their relationship with Islam."[109] In this case, he states:

> As we move into our discussion of the relationship between Islam and Black Religion, four key facts must be born in mind. First, the spread of Islam among Blackamericans was a twentieth-century phenomenon. Second, it was a northern phenomenon. Third, it was an urban phenomenon. And, finally, it was largely a working-class and underclass phenomenon.[110]

Jackson does not deny that there is some connection to that past or that there were Muslims among the enslaved brought to the Americas. But, since there was no sustained growth until the twentieth-century, the U.S. African American Muslim community has to be studied within its socio-historic location.

Both the point of going back to slavery in order to find connections and Jackson's argument of a more recent development help us put in perspective the process through which U.S. Latina/o Muslims re-construct their identities. Both challenge the perception that there is a "natural" connection between Christianity and Black religion. In the case of "going back" and re-interpreting the history of slavery through the lenses of Islam (historical consciousness), U.S. African American Muslims discover a cultural memory that makes sense and gives them cultural meaning, similarly to U.S. Latina/o Muslims do as they go back into the history of a Muslim Spain. On the other hand, by situating the community within the trajectory of Blackamerica, Jackson does not try to create a linear historical narrative about Islam and Black religion in the United States, but re-interpret the narratives that have been presented as normative in a coherent manner. I see Jackson making the history of Blackamericans messy in order to attain new connections with the past through the lenses of Islam, while at the same time breaking with what he calls the "false universal," which refers "to the phenomenon of history internalized, normalized, and then forgotten as history."[111] U.S. Latina/o Muslims, in re-constructing their identities, also challenge what may seem to them to be a false universal—the marriage between Christianity and Latina/o

---

109. Jackson, *Islam and the Blackamerican*, 40.

110. Ibid., 38–39.

111. Ibid., 9.

identities—by subverting the narrative by which they have been made normative.

In both cases it is matter of re-visiting historical narratives of a distant past or a more recent one. Their initial process, as we have introduced in this chapter, allows them to begin re-defining their culture and history. As Guillermo Araya Goubet states, "History achieves its full meaning only when it creates an adequate awareness of the past in a community that recognizes that past as its very own."[112] Only through the re-membering of the Islamic past and deconstruction of the normative narrative based on the colonial Catholic tradition can they see a history that actually makes sense, and is comprehensible from their social/cultural location. If U.S. Latina/o Muslims continue this re-defining, they will eventually get to look at other portions of the historical narratives with the suspicion that they too hide voices and memories. It is not unlikely that through the use of their re-created historical consciousness they will dis-cover new memories in the history of Latin America, memories that while present in some official histories may have been forgotten or hidden by the normative knowledge.[113] The fact is that whatever the re-interpretations bring forth they will continue to challenge the norm. The uncovered past becomes a lived experience and the source of the creation of identities that provide meaning to their conversion and culturally legitimizes their religious experiences. U.S. Latina/o Muslims argue that they should not be marginalized for what some perceive as them "going against" their own culture because they see themselves as essentially retrieving and then transforming that culture rather than abandoning it. Certainly it would take some time to construct clear U.S. Latina/o Muslim identities but through the dis-covery and the re-membering of the Islamic past, the path towards those identities is created, challenging the traditional understandings of U.S. Latina/o identities.

112. Araya Goubet, "The Evolution of Castro's Theories," 47.

113. One of those dis-covered memories that may serve U.S. Latina/o Muslims in their process of re-inventing their culture is the experience of Muslim enslaves in Latin America. For example, the history of Brazil cannot be narrated without telling the story about slave revolts, especially the one in 1835. As João José Reis states, "Beyond a shadow of a doubt, Muslims played the central role in the 1835 rebellion. The rebels went into the streets wearing clothes peculiar to practicers of Islam. And the police found Muslim amulets and papers with prayers and passages from the *Koran* on the bodies of fallen rebels." [Reis, *Slave Rebellion in Brazil*, 93.] This type of dis-covery provides U.S. Latina/o Muslims with another contact and connection with a cultural past, even if it is not part of a linear historical narrative.

4

Re-constructing: New U.S. Latina/o Identities

PHILOSOPHER JORGE J. E. Gracia certainly recognizes the importance of history in the process of identity construction among U.S. Latina/os when he states:

> This group of people must be understood as forming a unit which goes beyond political, territorial, linguistic, cultural, racial, or genetic frontiers. It is not even necessary that the members of the group name themselves in any particular way or have a consciousness of their identity. Some of them may in fact consider themselves Hispanic and even have a consciousness of their identity as a group, but it is not necessary that all of them do. Knowledge does not determine being. What ties them together, and separates them from others, is history and the particular events of that history rather than the consciousness of that history; a unique web of changing historical relations supplies their unity.[1]

Though as a historian I agree with the importance of history, Gracia's dismissal of the role of consciousness to my mind restricts the actual functionality of historical perspectives within a group's process of identity construction. While history provides representations of the past it is only through our understandings of those representations (historical consciousness) that we position ourselves within society and begin constructing the self (individually and collectively). The official narratives of the past are often developed through colonial discourses that silence voices and leave some people outside of the official history. In the case of U.S. Latina/os, these narratives are sustained by colonial discourses of history and race. Historical consciousness from a subaltern perspective, the perspective of the Other, breaks down those discourses and deconstructs the normative historical narratives by recognizing the ideology and purpose

1. Gracia, *Hispanic/Latino Identity*," 49.

behind them. Thus, identities are grounded within the *understandings* of history, not, as Gracia suggests, in the historical narrative per se.

We saw in the previous chapter that U.S. Latina/o Muslims use this type of historical consciousness: allows individuals and groups to re-interpret the historical narratives and also to dis-cover what is missing or has been silenced within these narratives. They use this re-constructed historical consciousness to dis-cover cultural memories with which they can then re-construct their identities independent of the stereotypes. Now, given that U.S. Latina/os in general are faced with the challenge of con-fronting the official narratives that locate them as Others within society and prevent them from constructing an identity independent from the labels and stereotypes the official history has constructed, how then do U.S. Latina/o Muslim in particular re-construct their identities in a way that fits within the larger U.S. Latina/o community? And how do these particularly Muslim identities challenge the more common understand-ings of U.S. Latina/o identities?

I address these issues in this chapter first by analyzing the ways in which U.S. Latina/os become Others within the larger U.S. society and how they use this liminal space or in-betweeness to tackle the labels and otherness produced by the normative historical narratives that have si-lenced their voices. For other U.S. Latina/o groups besides Muslims also use their religious experiences as means to dis-cover cultural memories that can contribute to their construction of identities independent of labels attached to them by the colonial discourses. By comparing and contrasting these processes we can locate U.S. Latina/o Muslims within the larger U.S. Latina/o community. Second, after this analysis, I examine how U.S. Latina/o Muslims' reconstruction of their identity informs the racialization of U.S. Latina/os, specifically how it challenges and trans-forms the traditional discourses of *mestizaje* developed by U.S. Latina/o religious scholars.

LATINA/OS AS OTHER IN THE UNITED STATES

Chief among the social discourses that fix identity in the United States of America is the myth of prosperity, justice, and freedom, exemplified by [U.S.] American exceptionalism and Manifest Destiny. This myth be-gan with understanding the land as virgin—which therefore necessarily meant eradicating Natives from its history—so that one could understand the "new" Americans as chosen people. This myth continues to ground the social, political, and religious activities of the nation, creating a mentality of "Us versus Them" which designates as Other everyone who does not fit the myth. The Other is typically the colonized, and is subjected to the control of those in power, the chosen people.

As an example of this, we recall that [U.S.] Native Americans were construed as barbarians and regressed peoples, and through that discursive construction (labeling) they became Others. Like the land (wilderness), so too non-natives deemed this people as needing to be conquered and tamed in order for the chosen ones to take over and claim what was "rightfully" theirs. The presence of this Other became essential in the development of the U.S. American myth, offering meaning to the process of identity construction by "Americans." Thus the dominant identity was developed in response to the presence of the Other; it is an identity based on what the Other is not. To the Other were attributed negative characteristics (such as being savage, lazy, irrational/crazy) so the dominant group could by default assume the opposite, positive characteristics. This myth of prosperity and freedom that sustains this colonial understanding of identity is still present in the United States today. As religious historian Daisy L. Machado argues, "We uncritically continue to hold onto a national self understanding which is necessarily embedded with the 'isms' of nationalism, racism, protectionism and individualism which continue to be part of the national mythology of the United States."[2]

Moreover, this system of self-identification has continued even as the "face" of the Other has changed. U.S. Latina/os have been considered Others since the "birth" of the nation in spite of the presence of *criollos* in the Southwestern region of North America. Euro-American attitudes toward the Mexicans were based upon the pre-existing racial conception of the superiority of the former. Thus, historian David J. Weber reminds us,

> Mexicans were described as lazy, ignorant, bigoted, superstitious, cheating, thieving, gambling, cruel, sinister, cowardly half-breeds. As a consequence of their supposed innate depravity, Mexicans were seen as incapable of developing republican institutions or achieving material progress. These opinions of Mexicans, some of which endure to the present, are familiar to most Southwesterners

2. Machado, "Of Borders and Margins," 32.

and can be found in the writing of many early Anglo-American writers.[3]

The Protestant missionary enterprise consequently directed itself to so-called un-civilized people who, the missionaries deemed, needed a stronger race to take them out of their wretchedness, ignorance, and degradation. Believing they could accomplish this by putting them in contact with the "American way of life," the missionaries endeavored to convert this people from a phase of supposed paganism and barbarity to Christianity.[4] The religious aspects of U.S. American Protestantism and the negative stereotypes imputed to Mexicans are closely related because these stereotypes were "based not so much on direct observation or experience with Mexicans, but was in large part an extension of negative attitudes toward Roman Catholic Spaniards which Anglo Americans had inherited from their Protestant English forebears."[5] Euro-Americans thus developed their racism against Mexicans before their actual contact and interaction with them.[6]

Considering them to be inheritors of Spaniards' attributes such as barbarity, Euro-Americans constructed Mexicans not only as Other but also as "inferior" Other as a way of sustaining their religious, social, economic, and political enterprises and conquests. Notions of the Mexican as stinking, sexually depraved, savage, and without the ability to progress shaped the message of the Protestant missionaries, a message deeply rooted in the ideology of Manifest Destiny. It is a message that continues to undergird relations with U.S. Latina/os in the present-day.

This construction of U.S. Latina/os as 'racialized' Other was not limited to military and religious debates in the Southwestern region of the nation, but was expanded by the military invasions and incursions by U.S. Americans in Cuba and Puerto Rico (the Spanish-Cuban War, later misrepresented as the Spanish-U.S. American War), and throughout the rest of the Americas in the second half of the twentieth century.[7] The national discussion regarding U.S. Latina/os as Other has once again increased in

3. Weber, *Myth and the History*," 153.

4. Martínez, "Origins and Development," 22–23.

5. Weber, 159.

6. De León, *They Called Them Greasers*; and Montejano, *Anglos and Mexicans.*

7. The issue of racialization of U.S. Latina/os will be fully discussed later in this chapter.

recent years because of the national debate regarding immigration and border security (meaning mainly immigration from and border security with Mexico). Latina/os have become outsiders, "illegals," those who take jobs away, and are "not from here." They fill the role of Other apparently necessary for construction of the national identity; it is a role that those in power have been deliberately pushing on U.S. Latina/os as a group—using colonial discourses of representation, and confining them to stereotypes and skewed definitions. Such colonial representations place U.S. Latina/os outside of the traditional historical narratives, as historical objects, obscuring their agency as historical subjects.

These colonial representations for the most part ignore the many national, cultural, historical, social, political, and linguistic differences among U.S. Latina/os, which deliberately results in the creation of a 'false image' that homogenizes U.S. Latina/os. What characterizes this homogenization is the act of naming the group as Hispanics, neglecting the linguistic diversity within our communities, and the racialization of minoritized groups in the country, which through categorization in a black/white paradigm leaves U.S. Latina/o differences hidden. Putting everybody within one group and naming is a way that those in power assume control over that group, which in turn makes it easier for them to impose their own systems on it. U.S. Latina/os live within the context of this process of colonization. Colonial representations affect the way we see ourselves as colonized people because they impose a colonial identity that in many cases defines our place within society.

It is only through U.S. Latina/os' deconstruction of these colonial representations and their establishment of self-identities that U.S. Latina/os can escape this characterization as Other. In the words of scholar Arturo J. Aldama, we therefore "challenge the violent practices of representation that reify our positions as barbarians, exotics, illegal aliens, addicts, primitives, criminals, and sexual deviants; the essentialist ways we are invented, simulated, consumed, vanished, and rendered invisible by the dominant culture; as well as the insidious processes of internalized colonialism in our understanding of ourselves and of others."[8] U.S. Latina/os can challenge the imposition of a colonial identity by recognizing that we live in the midst of those colonial constructions. Aldama continues: "The continual interplay of how we are invented, demonized, and vanished by the

8. Aldama, *Disrupting Savagism*," 3.

colonizing culture, and how we form ourselves as a result, is an effective way to understand the struggle for identity for peoples caught in historical and contemporary displacements of colonial and neocolonial violence."[9] This process of identity construction challenges the positioning of U.S. Latina/os as Other by confronting the imposition of a "false image," and the practices used to sustain it. By retrieving historical consciousness, we can recognize the variety within this group and deconstruct the homogenous depiction imposed by those in power.

U.S. LATINA/OS AS PEOPLE IN THE MIDDLE

In the process of constructing U.S. Latina/os as a homogenous Other within this nation, those in power subvert the historical consciousness of this group by insisting that the only significant historical narrative is the meta-narrative or all-encompassing myth those in power have imposed. The ideologies of this meta-narrative promote colonial representations in order to maintain the domination of a particular group. In the United States context, the history of U.S. Latina/os is important only to the extent that it fits within that meta-narrative; stories that do not fit or which challenge this meta-narrative are deliberately left outside of the official historical memory of the nation. Breaking down the meta-narrative, and thus the imposed colonial identity, can only be done by moving beyond the social identification of Latina/os as Other within the United States, and taking seriously Latina/os' social/cultural/historical relationships to Latin America. Of course, these are many, and vary by class, gender, race, and/or nationality, and so forth: we do of course need to be ware of homogenizing these Latin American perspectives too. The history and heritage of Latin America, as a region, complicate the condition of the Otherness of U.S. Latina/os as these become crucial sources for the construction of identities, different from the ones imposed by those in power and reproduced by their colonial representations, understanding these may not "fit" everyone.

For the majority of U.S. Latina/os, the process of self-identification begins in Latin America. The cultural heritage of their particular country shapes a particular identity. This is why most U.S. Latina/o will identify with their country of origin as they identify themselves. The legacies of European colonialisms and destruction of our indigenous groups, the

9. Ibid., 20.

imposition of a religion through the power of the sword, the search for de-colonization through the wars of independence, the totalitarian attitudes produced by the imposition of capitalism and the creation/solidification of elites, and the struggle for liberation and human rights in the last decades, are all intrinsic aspects of U.S. Latina/o identities. They speak to the history of struggle of people for a self-identity in Latin America. Thus, in the context of the United States, for the most part U.S. Latina/os see themselves as continuing to construct their identities as they live in-between a cultural history of struggle and the "new" condition of Otherness. It is a condition of liminality. As Latino scholar William V. Flores explains, "It is a border that both separates and links two worlds and we, with a foot on both sides, are both trapped and liberated, defined by others, yet free to define ourselves."[10] The shape and extent of this in-betweeness varies among U.S. Latina/os since the political and economic realities also vary by nationality, which in itself discredits the perception of homogenization those in power try to impose.

From this liminal place, U.S. Latina/os start to break down homogenization in favor of non-essentialized identities by challenging the racialization process in the United States, which is similar to the process we explained U.S. Latina/o Muslims go through within the larger U.S. Latina/o community. For identity in Latin America is differently understood from identity in the United States. Following a Marxist approach, identity in Latin America becomes an issue of class, as people and communities "acquire their identities through their relation to uneven development."[11] What this means is that class, while tied to race, should not necessarily be understood in light of the racial divide as typically happens in the United States. Moreover, as we will elucidate later, the traditional black/white paradigm in the United States does not "fit" the reality of Latin America. Instead, because of the history and legacy of social/economic oppression there, class is central to understanding identity in Latin America. The history of exclusion from the time of European colonization to the present-day reality of totalitarian governments has created class divisions within Latin American countries. From revolutionary independence movements against the colonial forces to insurrections by popular sectors of society against the elites' power to socio/religious movements like liberation

10. Flores, "Epilogue," 257.
11. Franco, "Latin American Intellectuals," 236.

theology and indigenous revolts like the Zapatista revolt in Chiapas, people have been struggling against the socio-economic divide, which in turn has brought them together in the construction of identities. These identities are not homogenous or static, for they are particular to a location and constantly changing, but their construction is based on the experience of marginalization and the class structure, not merely of the racial divide. The same is true of how Latina/os in the United States experience marginalization within that society.

Though multiple migration movements produce physical re-locations and personal transformations, U.S. Latina/os who have immigrated do not leave behind the identities they have developed.[12] On the contrary, these identities become building blocks for the development of diasporic identities. While in the United States the racial paradigm dominates the discussion of identity, U.S. Latina/os typically enter this discussion on race through their class structure because class is a familiar and common denominator. In this sense, U.S. Latina/os locate themselves between worlds as they construct their identities in a way that is distinctive from that imposed by colonial representations. They re-interpret their culture through independent historical consciousnesses as a way to construct identities and fit within society.

LOOKING THROUGH CULTURE

Normative understandings of membership in a society are measured by one's relationship to the mainstream. U.S. Latina/os struggle to be part of (or to challenge) the mainstream and acquire full citizenship. Beyond mere legal citizenship, I am focusing on the social and cultural aspects of citizenship, on acceptance and recognition of humanness in diversity. "Cultural citizenship refers to the right to be different (in terms of race, ethnicity, or native language) with respect to the norms of the dominant national community, without compromising one's right to belong, in the sense of participating in the nation-state's democratic processes."[13] This understanding is more relevant today than ever before because of the multiplicity of "legal" experiences of U.S. Latina/os who "range from na-

---

12. For most non-first generation U.S. Latina/os, these experiences of migration or national identity may not seem familiar or relevant, but this doesn't take away its importance to the processes of raising children and learning within the household.

13. Rosaldo and Flores, "Identity, Conflict," 57.

tive born (some families resident in the present territorial United States since the sixteenth century) through U.S. citizens born in their homeland (Chicanos and Puerto Ricans), and naturalized citizens, to recent immigrants who may be either legal or undocumented."[14] This expansion of the understanding of citizenship to cultural citizenship also "enables a deeper understanding of the social and cultural struggles" of particular groups, not just those divided by race or ethnicity.[15] So in the process of identity construction, beyond traditional and sometimes pointless discussions on race and ethnicity and beyond legal considerations of citizenship, it is culture, more than race or ethnicity, is the fundamental aspect explored by U.S. Latina/os in their process of identity construction because it not only allows individual reflection but also collective recognition of a community.[16]

Yet here too the need for fluidity and constant transformation applies to culture, for the use of culture as a background, even when it is changing, allows the colonized an opportunity to claim hybrid spaces. "Culture provides, then, a sense of belonging to a community, a feeling of entitlement, the energy to face everyday adversities, and a rationale for resistance to a larger world in which members of minority groups feel like aliens in spite of being citizens."[17] By finding a culture U.S. Latina/os also find a path towards self-identities, moving them away from imposed definitions, and allowing them to consider the multi-meanings of experiences that inform who they are beyond simplistic ethnic or racial identities. Recognizing culture and cultural citizenship moves U.S. Latina/os to break down their colonial representations as Other. The search for culture through the dis-covery of stories and experiences—that is, through the use of historical consciousness—this is the core in the construction of identities. We have already seen that this historical consciousness is differ-

14. Ibid., 59.

15. Benmayor et al., "Claiming Cultural Citizenship," 153.

16. My use of the concept community as a general term does not imply the essentialization of U.S. Latina/os as a group. Community as a term carries within it a complexity that cannot be reduced to one aspect but always includes many (e.g. race, ethnicity, class, gender, and family, among others). Here, I am using the term to argue that in order to acquire subjectivity, U.S. Latina/os find cultural connections among themselves that bring them together, even if for a short period of time, and create collective identities that challenge the colonial representations. Community is that "coming together."

17. Silvestrini, "The World We Enter," 43.

ent from the one imposed by the meta-narrative because it comes out of the in-betweeness, where the colonial representations do not fit.

We have already recognized that historical consciousness opens the way to look beyond the meta-narrative of imposed colonial representations. Whereas this meta-narrative offers answers but does not allow questioning, historical consciousness deconstructs the discourses embedded within the meta-narrative, rendering it useless. Historical consciousness "facilitates images from the soul and the unconscious through dreams and imagination."[18] I speak about this consciousness from a liminal space in the same way Chicana feminist Gloria Anzaldúa refers to the concept of *la facultad*, as "an acute awareness mediated by the part of the psyche that does not speak, that communicates in images and symbols which are the faces of feelings, that is, behind which feelings reside/hide."[19] U.S. Latina/os have this *facultad* because their condition as outcast, marginalized, and persecuted people awakens and increases this psychic awareness. They can dis-cover the past through new lenses, and in doing so their identity construction becomes a subversive practice, debunking the traditional and normative understanding of the past as fixed and finished. Culture allows a new vision of the self. Culture allows the colonized to situate themselves as part of their particular history. Religious experiences, in many cases, play an essential role in this process because they open the door for that cultural memory to serve as the basis for identities, independent from the labels. It brings people together, allowing them to remember.

RELIGION AS A SOURCE OF CULTURAL MEMORY

As U.S. Latina/o Muslim religious experiences prove, religion functions as one of those lived experience that advances the act of remembering and therefore the construction of identities. For U.S. Latina/os, religious experience "has always been an important element of their cultural fabric and ethnic identities."[20] Yet, religion is not a fixed characteristic; those experiencing it transform it constantly, making it always hybrid. However, religious experiences through rituals and practices not only acquire meaning throughout time but also may become tradition, which may seem to be fixed. In this sense, religion needs to be understood as a socio-cultural

18. Anzaldúa, *Borderlands/La Frontera*," 37.

19. Ibid., 38.

20. Cadena, "Religious Ethnic Identity," 33.

instrument, whose use depends on the social location of those experiencing it. It is a lived experience that speaks to the connection between the experience with God and the experience of a community, and for that matter acquires power—"but will it be a power unto life or a power of sacralized and legitimized oppression, margination, exclusion, ethnocide and even genocide?"[21] Differentiating between the kinds of power is essential because religious institutions, for the most part, have been responsible for establishing fixed religious traditions that preclude religious experiences and rituals as sources for dis-covering cultural memory. On the other hand, individuals and communities have stepped away many times from those institutionalized traditions and through the use of popular religion and local ritual have constructed identities distinct from the ones established by people in power.

By moving away from traditions imposed to isolate people, colonial subjects create rituals and experiences of faith that give meaning to their liminality. For example, in the history of Latin America the colonial subjects, both indigenous communities and enslaved Africans, created religious systems to confront the domination imposed by the colonizer. These religious systems, like Afro-Latin religions, generated in most cases through syncretic activities, proved to be essential for these groups' survival in the face of oppression and marginalization. Even in more recent history, religious experience is core in the creation of identities in Latin America. For example, by participating in the liberation theology movements and the Pentecostal movements Latin Americans have developed communal identities that have certainly helped bring people together even if they have not fixed. Religious experiences as lived experiences have become important in developing cultural identities among Latin Americans and this importance translates into the life of U.S. Latina/os.[22]

Religious experience gives meaning to colonial subjects' history of struggle while also opening the door for the development of identities that challenge the imposed identities and stereotypes. It opens the door for the dis-covery of historical consciousness. Not that religious experience only serves to challenge the system since it is clear that religion has been used within processes of colonization and assimilation. Rather, for

21. Elizondo, "Popular Religion as the Core," 114.

22. This primary role of religious experience in the construction of cultural identities is not specific to U.S. Latina/os as it also applies to other racial/ethnic groups in the United States (e.g. U.S. African Americans and U.S. Irish Americans).

the most part, colonial subjects, people in the middle, see religious experience as a mode of liberation, reinforcing a cultural memory and building cultural identities. This process happens in community as colonial subjects look at religious experience not only in light of the relationship with a higher being but also of that between individuals. Religion brings a community together in the construction of the self. It gives people a sense of belonging and a communal experience with a higher power, and it also helps them reconstruct an identity based both on the religious past and on communal experiences Moreover in the context of people living in the middle, "Religious experience interprets the way a community defines the world, and it does so in such a way that establishes its primary values, affects, behaviors, and choices."[23]

U.S. Latina/os experience religion in this way as they become involved in communal rituals and acquire symbols that articulate their opposition and resistance to the discourses that fix identity. These rituals and symbols become aspects of cultural memory. They provide the opportunity to "remember," to dis-cover the history that may have been silenced by colonial interpretations of the past. They give meaning to the community as the community assigns meaning to them. In the words of Catholic theologian Virgilio Elizondo,

> These religious practices are the ultimate foundation of the people's innermost being and the common expression of their collective soul. They are supremely meaningful for the people who celebrate them, but often appear meaningless to the outsider. To the people whose very life-source they are, no explanation is necessary, but to the casual spectator no explanation will ever express or communicate their full meaning. Without them, there might be associations of individuals bound together by common interest (e.g. the corporation, the state, etc . . .), but there will never be the experience of being a people, *un pueblo*.[24]

Religious experiences open up the imagination of the community to new identities, as these experiences become cultural processes that bring together historical memories and everyday life experiences. Through them U.S. Latina/os are empowered to develop new religious meanings. As one Mexican American anthropologist suggests, "The self-creation of Latino community with its own set of religious meanings represents a process

23. Ibid.
24. Elizondo, 117.

that constitutes social power and cultural identity that jeopardizes the political power of the church."[25]

As people in the middle, Latina/os in the United States look to religion to challenge their sense of otherness—by looking beyond the traditional understandings of history and knowledge, by jeopardizing the power of the social and cultural system that silences the voices of these communities and labels them. For by engaging religion, U.S. Latina/os re-visit symbols, images, and rituals that provide an opening to the discovery of alternative knowledges, both religious and also simply cultural, which help them retrieve historical cultural memories and identities and thus self identities.

In the next few pages, we look at two U.S. Latina/o Christian communities in Miami and Washington D.C. that through their religious experiences are able to dis-cover cultural memories and, thus, develop cultural identities. In these examples it is clear that religious experiences, evidenced in the establishment of symbols and rituals, are grounded in a communal act of remembering, which at the same time is based on a re-interpretation of the past that challenges the present conditions of liminality. The meanings communities assign to the symbols and the rituals legitimize these re-interpretations that lead to that development of cultural identities.

Finally, we compare and contrast the way these two communities use their religious experiences as a source for cultural memories with the way U.S. Latina/o Muslims use it.

Cuban Community in Miami

Though it has become a city of immigrants from multiple nations, Miami is still commonly identified as "Little Havana," in reference to its large population of Cuban immigrants. A detailed analysis of the Cuban reality in Cuba and Miami lies outside the scope of my project. Instead, I focus on the way Cubans construct their identity in relation to religion, and specifically to the symbol of Our Lady of Charity. In his 1997 study regarding the role of this religious symbol as a national symbol, Thomas A. Tweed analyzes the way diasporic religion serves the Cuban community in negotiating identities. This negotiating is part of the process of

---

25. Flores, "Para El Niño Dios," 184.

remembering and serves as an example of how religion allows for the construction of cultural identities within the experiences of liminality.

Cubans in Miami in their constant search for identity in exile have turned to religion and especially to the symbol of Our Lady of Charity. While Tweed offers multiple explanations for Miami Cubans' adherence to the Catholic Church, he acknowledges that the explanation favored by most devotees of the Virgin is that "there is something about the disorientation and suffering of exile itself that has led them to religion."[26] In the words of one of Tweed's interviewees, "Cubans in Miami turn to religion more because they have suffered more."[27] This observation fits with my earlier description of how colonial subjects in light of liminality look at religious experiences as a source for constructing identity. In light of this approach, Cubans in Miami experience religion as a socio-cultural instrument that helps them make sense of their social location and its relation to the past. Our Lady of Charity, thus, becomes a cultural artifact as much as it is a religious symbol.

This symbol in no way has a predetermined meaning; different communities may assign their own meanings, as the Christian construction of the Virgin and Afro-Latin construction of Ogún—the *orisha* represented by the image of the Virgin—exemplify. These multiple narratives have positioned this symbol at the center of a national identity among this diasporic community. As Tweed points out, "the biography of the Virgin and the history of the nation are so connected that they seem indistinguishable."[28] In other words, this religious symbol has become a national symbol that provides this displaced community with an opportunity to remember their history back on the island and in their present situation in the diaspora. The construction of identity around this religious symbol is what links "the collective identity of the Cuban diaspora and the fate of the island nation."[29] The multiple and contested meanings of the symbol of Our Lady of Charity, and the shrine dedicated to it, puts in perspective that, "the struggles over *national* identity in many ways are more important than those over *religious* identity, although the two are

26. Tweed, *Our Lady of the Exile*, 31.
27. Ibid.
28. Ibid., 32.
29. Ibid., 31.

related."[30] Indeed, this religious symbol has become a cultural artifact that prompts people to dis-cover cultural memories and construct a cultural identity. It is the community rather than the institution of the Catholic Church that defines the symbol and assigns it multiple meanings. Thus, the community sees this contested religious symbol not simply as a communal experience with a higher power, but as a cultural artifact that facilitates the re-construction of an identity based on their communal historical consciousness as well as their religious past. The historical foundation of these meanings provides a solid basis for constructing cultural identities that move beyond those promoted by those in power.

Salvadoran Communities in Washington D.C.

Salvadorans began seeking asylum in the United States as a result of civil war, persecution, and for economic reasons. Washington D.C. was the destination of one of the largest influxes of these Salvadoran migrant communities. In the same way that Cuban exiles in Miami draw upon their religious experiences and the symbol of Our Lady of Charity in developing their cultural identities, Salvadorans understand the intrinsic relation between their religious experiences and their historical consciousness. This relationship is based on the importance Salvadorans put on the development of a social agenda, ground in what Harold Recinos calls "the religion of martyrology," which "relates belief in a God who sides with the poor and those classified as social martyrs to the struggle to end human rights violations, the democratization of the state, the demilitarization of society, and the achievement of economic justice."[31] Salvadorans find their cultural identities by assigning meaning to the symbol of "social martyrs," and as they practice the Liberation Mass.

In the context of liminality, Salvadorans look to their national past by re-interpreting that history and dis-covering the cultural memory embedded within that past. We do well to understand the development of this cultural memory in the context of liberation theology, as it is within this context that the socio-religious call for change happened. The Liberation Mass, developed as a ritual that includes a call for social change, is a source of identity for these faith communities. As Recinos notes, "Developed in the context of political resistance, the Liberation Mass fixes the religious

30. Ibid., 44.

31. Recinos, "Mainline Hispanic Protestantism," 195.

identity of members of these churches in a culture of opposition whose nucleus is the historical struggle of El Salvador's subaltern classes."[32] This "religious identity is decisively affixed to belief in a God who clarifies the project of the poor, which means favoring life, human rights, economic redistribution, and democratic values for government."[33] Because this ritual is grounded in a socio-historical interpretation of the past it speaks both to a religious identity and a cultural identity.

The liturgy of the Liberation Mass acquires religious meanings as well as historical, political, social, and cultural meanings, particularly through the subversive remembering of "social martyrs." Salvadorans through the religious activity of liturgy and the remembrance of the "social martyrs" construct a self-identity based on their historical consciousness in addition to the Christian experience. This self-identity is no longer the imposed one, but one which subversive memory revises and refreshes.

Subversive memory, the act of remembering outside the established contours of normative knowledge, helps the Salvadoran community to see beyond the official narratives assigned them by the government of El Salvador. The religious practices of this refugee community allow that subversive memory to serve as an interpretative lens of their situation, beginning with the self-recognition of their socio-economic location, thus validating the oppositional character of their religious experience and the construction of a cultural memory that counters the labeling. Recinos describes and analyzes two religious activities that help clarify this argument. The first one is the act of reading the Bible. "By reading the Bible from the perspective of the poor, made concrete by their own liminal status as refugees and by the memory of their social martyrs, these Salvadorans, who associated with a mainline Hispanic Protestant church, have demarginalized themselves, erected community as an alternative response to powerlessness, and invented their refugee group as a social force in the context of the barrio."[34] This common religious activity, which may seem innocent and even trivial, becomes subversive by being done from an oppositional location for it reaffirms the authority that lies within the community rather than the one outside. The second example is quite different. "Popular songs developed in the context of Salvadoran political

32. Ibid., 201.
33. Ibid., 205.
34. Ibid., 198.

struggle are used to keep alive the sentiment of revolt, and the commitment to unity and organized political encounter."[35] These "function as
ritual structures that generate and reinforce a political self-identity in the
context of a culture of struggle."[36] These two examples prove the importance of religious experiences in the construction of cultural identities as
the community participates in them out of their commitment not only to
God, but also to the development of their own selves.

The liturgy of the Liberation Mass, the reading of the Bible from the
perspective of the poor, the singing of popular songs, and the remembrance of the "social martyrs" are not only religious activities but also
cultural productions. These activities provide the community with an opportunity to come together and challenge the broken memories created
by oppression and the location of being in the middle. These symbols and
rituals work in a subversive way challenging the domination of those in
power. Through them the Salvadoran community can define itself and
build a cultural identity grounded in the experience of the people and
their historical past.

Comparing Types of Cultural Memories

The historical narratives that serve as the source for labeling and stereotyping create normative knowledges that in some ways are seen as the truth.
It creates a colonial imaginary that then becomes the lens through which
the past is read and interpreted. The colonial imaginary is responsible
for the development of a historical consciousness that does not recognize
the subjecthood of the people outside of the narratives. But, communities—and in this case U.S. Latina/os—find holes within the traditional
narratives they are able to dis-cover the forgotten/broken memories in
those spaces. The symbols of Our Lady of Charity and the social martyrs
are located in these spaces, not as part of the traditional/normative historical narrative. Cubans and Salvadorans dis-cover them, respectively, in
order to restore a historical consciousness that may have been lost with
the struggle of migrations. Thus, while the normative narratives build a
colonial historical consciousness filled with forgotten memories (holes),
through the use of cultural memory as a subversive practice, communities
are able to deconstruct the narratives and the consciousness it creates and

35. Ibid., 199.
36. Ibid.

engage in a process of self-identification. Through their religious experiences, which should be considered cultural practices, members of these communities were able to re-member and build cultural identities based on a dis-covered historical consciousness. In both cases, the community turned to a symbol that allowed them to "not forget" its cultural past and to confront the normative narratives imposed by those in power.

U.S. Latina/o Muslims follow the same process of decolonization, using cultural memory as a subversive activity, but there are significant differences in the way it is developed. The most recognizable differences have to do with the type of dis-covered memories. While Cuban and Salvadorans' memories come from a recent past and are intrinsically related to national identity, the ones dis-covered by U.S. Latina/o Muslims come from long ago and are not specific to a particular nationality but to larger context. One the other hand, these differences do not fully explain the most distinctive divergence between the processes, which lies within the actual act of re-membering. The Cuban and Salvadoran communities employ cultural memory as a way not to forget their history amidst the dominant culture's intent of silencing their voices and hiding their stories through the imposition of a colonial imaginary. The religious experiences that support the act of re-membering present the possibility of understanding symbols and rituals as lived experiences and thus open the door for the construction of cultural identities outside of the colonial imaginary. In the case of U.S. Latina/o Muslims, cultural memory also results in the construction of cultural identities (or at least in the development of the process for it); it does not lead in the same direction as for Cuban and Salvadorans.

After conversion, U.S. Latina/o Muslims are left in a liminal space because they are seen as Others even within their own communities.[37] Forced to search for a way to respond to this feeling, they explore the historical narratives that have dominated the discourses of identity. They find that within the normative and official narratives stories have been hidden and memories been buried in an effort to construct a linear discourse that privileges one particular group, in this case Catholicism. These holes in the narratives are not broken memories that need to be mended, but memories that in so many ways have been concealed as significant aspects in the construction of a historical consciousness. Thus, U.S.

---

37. Of course, this liminality is beyond the initial liminal space they occupy as a consequence of being Latina/os in the United States.

Latina/o Muslims first need to dis-cover these memories (which means going back) in order then to move to the act of re-membering (putting it together) as they attempt to re-construct their identities. The complication with re-construction of identities as they use cultural memory is that the memories have to fit the new positioning of the community as Muslim and Latina/o. The dis-covery of Muslim Spain allows them the possibility of actual recognition and self-identities that fit within both groups.

The U.S. Latina/o Muslims' process of cultural memory is no tougher than the one Cubans and Salvadorans go through. The processes are simply different in the ways they are implemented and the needs that they address. One of them moves from re-membering to challenging the normative discourses and the other begins with the opening of the official narratives, dis-covers its silences, and dismantles the narrative's apparent linearity. On the other hand, both are pressured by a situation of Otherness and in-betweeness and both serve as conduits to the construction of identities, specifically non-fixed hybrid cultural identities. Cultural identity as an act of re-membering opens the door so these communities can experience their religious and social symbols and their dis-covered memories as part of their lived religions. This means that Our Lady of Charity and the social martyrs, as symbols, and likewise the dis-covered Islamic traditions embedded within the historical consciousness of U.S. Latina/os, are not simple unchanging artifacts or stories in a distant past. Instead, their power exposed through cultural memory is lived out in the religious experiences of these communities. Because of these similarities, it is important to include the perspective of U.S. Latina/o Muslims in the wider discourses of U.S. Latina/o religious experiences and examine the way Muslims' re-construction of identities affects the overall understanding of U.S. Latina/o identities. Thus, U.S. Latina/o Muslims' process fits the general model of identity construction of other U.S. Latina/o groups. Yet these voices have been absent from the discourses in U.S. Latina/o studies and especially in U.S. Latina/o theology and religious studies. Their inclusion contests the U.S. Latina/o identities that have been essentialized by these discourses, exposing these discourses as limited. One of the issues within the discourses that get exposed as limited is the racialization of U.S. Latina/o identities.

RACIALIZATION OF U.S. LATINA/O IDENTITIES

As we have mentioned before this condition of in-betweeness in which U.S. Latina/os find themselves results in the creation of hybrid identities—"new transcultural forms within the contact zone produced by colonization."[38] Hybridity comes out of a contact and exchange between the colonizer and the colonized. U.S. Latina/o cultural identities are the result of multiple process of hybridity, in the construction of Latin American identities and in the development of new identities in the United States. With the inclusion of the perspective put forward by U.S. Latina/o Muslims, one should add the contact and exchange in Spain as part of the multiple hybrid processes. These constructions of identities thus locate U.S. Latina/os in that in-between space where culture and identity are always in flux, never fixed and pure. From this space, one can read history differently and deconstruct the meta-narrative that imposes meanings and identities upon colonial subjects.

Yet essentializing hybridity and in-betweeness "fails to discriminate between the diverse modalities of hybridity, for example, forced assimilation, internalized self-rejection, political cooptation, social conformism, cultural mimicry, and creative transcendence."[39] The condition of hybridity allows U.S. Latina/os, as colonial subjects, to either assimilate to the dominant culture and its colonial representations or to resist the domination of these representations. I am arguing that through the use of historical consciousness, U.S. Latina/os locate themselves as a collective resisting the fixing of their identity by challenging dominant historical discourses and dis-covering the histories of their hybrid identities. Challenging historical discourses allows them to initiate a process for self-identification disassociated from the fixed labels embedded within the traditional colonial discourses of race.

Mestizaje is the term coined to reflect upon U.S. Latina/os hybrid identities. The problem is that *mestizaje* has become an "all-encompassing" term to define the condition of hybridity, and it has essentialized this condition among U.S. Latina/os. It responds to the process of categorization by those in power in order to fix an alternative racial construct. This essentializing hides the multiplicity of experiences or mixtures that comprise this hybridity in Latin American countries by focusing on the

38. Ashcroft et al., *Post-Colonial Studies*, 118.

39. Shohat, "Notes on the 'Post-Colonial,'" 331.

finished product and leaving behind the particular characteristics of the mixing, or simply by focusing on one characteristic over others. This type of mentality erases stories in order to posit a new (uncomplicated) being. For example, the racialization of U.S. Latina/os through *mestizaje* has to be understood in light of racial constructions from Latin America that are based on hierarchies and domination. Tomás Almaguer explains the complexity of these racial constructions:

> There are profound historical factors that account for this unique mapping of race among Latinos/as in the United States. Their multiracial composition has its roots in Spanish colonialism during which the colonial states imposed racial hierarchies that were more gradational and fluid in nature than in their northern counterparts. More so than in the English colonies, Spanish colonization in Cuba, Mexico, Puerto Rico, and elsewhere in Latin America entailed widespread miscegenation among the Spanish, Indian, and African populations. The racial order in Mexico, for example, where the colonized Indians composed the most subordinate racial group and principal labor force, was organized primarily around Spanish/Indian miscegenation. The racial order in the Caribbean, on the other hand, where African slaves assumed the most subordinate position, was organized in Spanish/African terms. These historical patterns, in addition to the differences in the timing of the subsequent colonization by the United States in the mid- and late nineteenth century, have factored centrally in the complex reracialization of the Latino/a population in the contemporary United States. These patterns, in turn, have important implications for the life chances of Latinos/as within the racial hierarchy and in varied social location due to other lines of group difference.[40]

Even this detailed description fails to grasp the hybrid complexities already embedded in the Spaniards conquistadores after the period of a Muslim Spain. These complexities tend to be erased through the essentialization of a racial identity for all U.S. Latina/os, and mestizaje has tended to be used as that essentializing concept. For people in power this process is of great service for it essentializes U.S. Latina/os in the "now" and erases their history, which of course facilitates the process of assimilation of these groups into the national agenda.

Because of the constant movement of U.S. Latina/os across the Americas through the different migration processes, we can only get snap-

40. Almaguer, "At the Crossroads of Race," 209.

shots of this hybridity in constant transformation. We best understand *mestizaje* as a complex condition of hybridity in light of the multiplicity of stories and experiences embedded within it. It means recognizing that people live in-between worlds while at the same time belonging in neither. The expression *No soy de aquí, ni soy de allá* [I am not from here, nor am I from there], coined by Latin American *trovador* Facundo Cabral in one of his songs, exemplifies this complexity. By instead claiming their own space, U.S. Latina/os accept their hybrid identities as in-betweeness (liminality) rather than as fixed identities, and establish themselves in direct contrast to those in power. Aldama acknowledges the importance of this process since, "By de/constructing or de/colonizing our subjectivities as hybrid, *mestiza/o*, and indigenous peoples, we can resist and disrupt different loci of social power and begin to understand ourselves as bordered and multiple beings who can draw on different reservoirs of signifying practices."[41]

Mestizaje can only be seen as a non-colonial representation if it is understood in light of these multiplicities outside of the social power (meta-narrative) of which Aldama speaks. U.S. Latina/os, thus, can confront labeling and its concomitant mis-representations by recognizing that their hybrid identities, their *mestizaje*, has a history and that it comes from somewhere and is not created in a vacuum. For example, the racial understandings brought from Latin America are combined with those racial definitions in the United States. This "situation reflects a clash between two cultures of race, as a Latino/a population, racialized according to one racial regime, is reracialized in the United States according to a different racial logic."[42] Within this context, U.S. Latina/os are actively engaged in the search for cultural memories that help them understand these conceptualizations of their racial identities. This is why an understanding of *mestizaje* cannot be essentialized but is always problematized, which is what U.S. Latina/o Muslim's dis-covered cultural memories provide. Nowhere does this problematization make more sense than in how U.S. Latina/o religious studies uses the concept *mestizaje*.

41. Aldama, 33.

42. Almaguer, 213. For a broad analysis on the historicity of the concept of *mestizaje*, including its dangers, see Vásquez, "Rethinking *Mestizaje*."

Reconceptualizing Mestizaje

U.S. Latina/o theologies and other fields within U.S. Latina/o religious studies have been responsible for the construction of the discourses that examine the relationships between religious experiences and U.S. Latina/o identities. These identities are created through oppositional consciousness, against the normative discourses of those in power, and they demonstrate the subjecthood of U.S. Latina/os even when they have been constructed as Other by the colonial imaginary. It results in the creation of identities that appear to have liberatory nature, a decolonial character. The problem is that in the process of constructing these identities most discourses within U.S. Latina/o religious studies have privileged some sources over others to the point of obscuring memories. The most recognizable aspect of this process is the focus on Christian religious experiences, leaving those non-Christian U.S. Latina/o religious communities outside of the imaginary it creates. Thus, these discourses, created as counter discourses through subversive practices acquired a new normativity as they essentialized U.S. Latina/o identities. While these counter discourses try to transform the normative discourses there is always a danger of the re-inscription of the same categories, and not necessarily completely break the boundaries.

Even if the ideology behind these constructions is not colonial, the actual discourses it creates seem colonial in that they are responsible for covering and silencing voices that break the normative character of the imaginary. Cuban theologian Michelle González argues that U.S. Latina/o scholars of religion have focused on the importance of culture "as the unifying element that links Latino/a peoples."[43] For González, this "emphasis on culture erases the diversity of the histories of Latino/a peoples and makes the experience of Spanish colonialism the thread that unites them."[44] Even when these discourses speak about difference they are closed to some differences that do not fit within the traditional historical consciousness. This is why, as Miguel De La Torre finds, it is important "to unmask how power operates within our own marginalized group, a re-

---

43. González, *Afro-Cuban Theology*, 9.

44. Ibid. While I agree with González' assessment, I find that it is not simply their emphasis on culture, but the understanding of culture as something fixed. This is different to my argument that culture should be a guiding point to the construction of identities because I see culture as fluid and ever-changing, not fixed in some particular past or tradition.

thinking is required—not just a rethinking of our religious concepts but, just as important, a rethinking of how we construct our very identity."[45]

For the most part, U.S. Latina/o scholars begin their analysis of U.S. Latina/o identities by examining the history of the conquest of the Americas, privileging the colonization of indigenous populations and thus neglecting the presence of Muslim traditions, as well as the history of the African slave trade. Michelle González in her analysis of U.S. Latina/o theology critiques the discourse within the field for this focus that "has become normative" even though it does not represent the totality of the diversity since "Not all of our foremothers and forefathers were conquered."[46] González is interested in deconstructing the discourses in light of its silences about the African elements that help build U.S. Latina/o heritage. She argues that because of its African roots, the symbol of Our Lady of Charity not only serves as a source for the construction of Cuban identity, it also underscores the significance of Africa in the construction of U.S. Latina/o identities. At the same time, she finds that one of the major problems with U.S. Latina/o theologies is that it has put at the center of its narrative Mexican American traditions to the point that, for example, the symbol of Our Lady of Guadalupe has become a normative representation of *latinidad*. This emphasis is nowhere more evident than in the understanding and use of the concept of *mestizaje* as a way to construct U.S. Latina/o identities.

So while *mestizaje* is used to define the hybrid condition of U.S. Latina/os, as an all-encompassing concept it hides some of the aspects that make up for the hybridity. In U.S. Latina/o religious studies, *mestizaje* seems to acquire this all-encompassing attribute and thus needs to be deconstructed and open to those aspects that have been covered as the identities are essentialized. The influence of Mexican American traditions within this conception of *mestizaje* can be traced to the work of Mexican philosopher José Vasconcelos, and "the writings of one of the founders of [U.S.] Latino/a theology, Virgilio Elizondo."[47] Both not only offer a romantic view of the hybrid reality (as chosen people) but also limit the understanding of this concept, not fully problematizing its complexity.

---

45. De La Torre, "Religion and Power," 288.
46. González, 22.
47. Ibid., 24.

In this concept, Elizondo sees hope for U.S. Latina/os who have the promise of "a new creative universal subject."[48] This promise is based on the challenge subaltern groups present to those in power because they break the normative understandings of racial purity, and Elizondo finds that the best representative of this process is Jesus, because as a Galilean, Jesus "was himself *mestizo*, laboring at a crossroads of peoples and cultures at the margins of the empire to build a new, inclusive reign of God."[49] In this sense, for Elizondo and other U.S. Latina/o religious scholars, *mestizaje* carries a theological meaning beyond its racial component. Manuel A. Vásquez, in his reading of Elizondo, goes further by arguing that because Elizondo understands *mestizaje* "through the lenses of liberationist Christianity," this concept "is not the inalienable property of Ibero-American civilizations or any other ethnic or national group, but the core of humanity itself."[50] Thus, *mestizaje* has not only a theological meaning but also a humanistic aspect. It is not founded in racial essentialism, as it actually challenges the racial constructions put forward by those in power, sustained by colonial discourses of racial purity and hierarchy that locate one race over another. Because of this function, *mestizaje* has become a core idea within U.S. Latina/o religious studies. Ethicist Ada María Isasi-Díaz states:

> In our theological endeavors, *mestizaje/mulatez* constitutes our *locus theologicus*—the place from which we do theology precisely because it is intrinsic to who we are. It situates us as a community in U.S. society. *Mestizaje/mulatez* is so important to us that we have suggested it as an ethical option, because it has to do with an understanding of difference that is intrinsic not only to the Latina community's identity but to everyone's sense of self.[51]

For many scholars within the field of U.S. religious studies, *mestizaje* is defined through an understanding of the religious experiences of U.S. Latina/os. For example, "For Elizondo, the Christian faith plays a central role in what *mestizaje* is, means, and signifies."[52]

---

48. Vásquez, "Rethinking *Mestizaje*," 139.

49. Ibid. Also see Elizondo, *Galilean Journey*.

50. Ibid., 140.

51. Isasi-Díaz, "A New Mestizaje/Mulatez," 204.

52. Ibid., 207.

Others go beyond the traditional Christian understandings in order to include the popular religious experiences, not simply the institutional perspectives. Isasi-Díaz, in her scrutiny and reconceptualization of this concept from a *mujerista* perspective, states that,

> In *mujerista* theology we have proposed an understanding of popular religion as a form of *mestizaje* in itself, as well as a key factor of *mestizaje* at large. We also recognize that both African and Amerindian religious understandings and practices are intrinsic elements of popular religion as well as of *mestizaje*. Our intention has been to broaden *mestizaje* to include African cultural, historical, and biological elements.[53]

In order to achieve this broadening of the concept, Isasi-Díaz and others "started to add *mulatez*—which refers to the mixing of the white and black races—to *mestizaje* instead of including our African heritage under this term."[54] These re-positions the sole focus of the term away from the Mexican American experience, as Vasconcelos and Elizondo appear to be doing, and includes a broader perspective, in this case the African heritage that is so prevalent in the Caribbean.

The conceptualization of *mestizaje* has gone through many transformations. While it may seem that the inclusion of multiple perspectives illustrates difference, the continuous and exclusive focus on this concept as an all-encompassing term is in part responsible for the homogenization of its meaning and has prevented U.S. Latina/o scholars from looking beyond essentialized U.S. Latina/o identities. For example, the most common understandings of *mestizaje*, before the addition of *mulatez*, did not integrate the histories of those groups outside of the story of the colonization of the Americas to the point of silencing them, as in the case of Africans, and erasing them, as in the case of Muslims. *Mestizaje* understood in this narrow way creates a colonial discourse, as U.S. Latina/o peoples that do not fit the discourse become Others. Even with the addition of *mulatez*, which Michelle González shows has not been fully integrated within U.S. Latina/o religious studies, the discourse of *mestizaje* is not open to difference, because it is not simply adding perspectives that will get lost in an homogenizing concept but actually having a concept (or concepts) that fully elucidate difference.

53. Ibid., 208.
54. Ibid.

Rather than advocate for the elimination of the term I want to show how the U.S. Latina/o Muslim perspective opens the concept of *mestizaje* to a larger perspective, breaking its colonial feature. For example, Vásquez states that *mestizaje* "helps Latinos to recover and celebrate the richness of their religious and cultural resources."[55] Yet its actual use within U.S. Latina/o religious studies has fallen short of providing this opportunity. The richness that can be recovered from the present understandings of *mestizaje* is based on a Christian paradigm and/or a relationship to it, as in the case of Afro-Caribbean religious experiences. Those outside of this limited richness become Other, like U.S. Latina/o Muslims.

While U.S. Latina/o Muslims in their process of re-construction of identities do not deny the importance of this history, they do challenge its primacy. By "going back," U.S. Latina/o Muslims alter this historical consciousness and expose the silences within the narratives and thus deconstruct the type of *mestizaje* that is based on a Christian paradigm. Islam takes "center stage," history is re-visited, and the normative discourses are broken as memories are dis-covered. The work of Raúl Gómez-Ruiz is important in this process of dis-covery for U.S. Latina/o religious studies because it reveals the connection between Iberian Peninsula and U.S. Latina/os beyond the limited focus on Catholicism. He writes about the link between Mozarab rituals and U.S. Latina/o Catholicism rituals. Because "[o]ne way that culture, identity, and therefore community develop is through rituals," he finds that the roots of the U.S. Latina/o liturgy in Spanish history should be considered part of the construction of U.S. Latina/o cultural identities.[56]

Other than Gómez-Ruiz, to date few U.S. Latina/o scholars have paid attention to Iberian history before 1492. Historian Alberto Hernández, talking about Gómez-Ruiz work, states:

> Thus, Gómez-Ruiz succeeds in showing us that Hispanic Christians, regardless of their contemporary Latin American stereotypes or North American racial profiling, also possess a story rooted in the early medieval cradle of European ethnic and religious culture. Hispanics, Latinos, and Latinas are not merely "recent arrivals" on the stage of Western civilization. Their story is not merely that of an insignificant "recent history," but is rather a

---

55. Vásquez, 142.

56. Gómez-Ruiz, "Ritual and the Construction," 9. Also see Gómez-Ruiz, *Mozarabs, Hispanics, and the Cross.*

story rooted in the dynamic multicultural tensions of the Iberian Peninsula, which long before 1492 functioned as the creative and progressive frontier of numerous Western European religious and intellectual currents.[57]

Like Michelle González, Raúl Gómez-Ruiz is interested in transforming the way U.S. Latina/o cultural identities have been constructed by enhancing the discourses. He understands not only that "many [U.S.] Latinas/os have only a faint and/or dismissive sense of their connection to Iberia," but that the effects of this "heritage are often underrepresented or ignored in the works written by [U.S.] Latina/o theologians."[58] So while this dis-covery triggers "the Hispanicization of [U.S.] Latina/o identity"[59] it also opens the discourses of identities and *mestizaje* to Islamic tradition, which is exactly U.S. Latina/o Muslims' purpose as they use cultural memory as a subversive activity.

By dis-covering the memories of Muslim Spain and breaking the linearity of the history, the colonial discourses (e.g. *mestizaje*) are deconstructed. U.S. Latina/o identities can no longer be homogenized through the use of a *mestizaje* that only takes into consideration a Spanish legacy that moreover only focuses on its Catholic experience. Thus, the racialization of U.S. Latina/o identities, exemplified by the use of *mestizaje*, cannot dismiss the hybridity that happened in Muslim Spain because the Spanish legacy that is fundamental in the construction of this racialization is founded upon this hybridity. The dis-covery of the cultural memories of this hybrid experience not only problematizes the discourses of *mestizaje* but also carries cultural meanings that then guide the construction of cultural identities. In this case, I agree with the usefulness of *mestizaje* as a concept within the parameters for which Manuel Vásquez argues. He states that, "*Mestizaje* can continue as a viable metaphor only if this cluster of discourses is historicized, contextualized, and relativized, that is, confronted at all times with the otherness that it contains and fails to contain."[60] This approach to *mestizaje* will not only continue to serve U.S. Latina/os in the confrontation of normative constructions of race; it will also avoid the temptation of seeing *mestizaje* in an homogenizing way

57. Hernández, "Hispanic Cultural Identity," 48.

58. Ibid., 36.

59. Ibid.

60. Vásquez, 149.

that includes differences yet erases them in favor of a universalized condition. *Mestizaje* must remain open to re-conceptualization, and in our case include U.S. Latina/o Muslims.

Afterword

Latinidades

T HE PURPOSE OF THIS book is not to fix the parameters of U.S. Latina/o identities, but to expose the way U.S. Latina/o Muslims are forced to confront the coloniality implicit in present discourses of U.S. Latina/o identities and how their process of re-construction of identities informs new conceptualizations about *latinidades*. Not to speak about U.S. Latina/o identities—*latinidades*—and continue perpetuating an imaginary that leaves people without a voice would be to reproduce the same discourses that they confront. As Michelle González argues, "We cannot afford to erase and marginalize portions of our population in favor of a more generalized description of our identity. To do so is to do violence to the communities we ignore and forget."[1] Thus, the deconstruction of traditional discourses and the incorporation of U.S. Latina/o Muslims' cultural memories, among others, while it does not complete the discourses, does increase the diversity and difference needed to re-construct U.S. Latina/o identities. Such deconstruction dis-covers the multiplicity of voices through new historical consciousness, which in turn serve as a foundation for constructing cultural identities. This process entails including new voices, silenced voices, even though "The construction of identity, whether cultural, racial, or ecclesial, is nonetheless an exclusionary process where one group's identity is set apart from that of the other group."[2] In this construction, one has to see cultural identities as fluid and ever changing, always open to dis-covered memories. As we saw in the previous chapter, this is evident in the way we must re-conceptualize the discourses of *mestizaje*, as open and not fixed.

---

1. González, *Afro-Cuban Theology*, 32.
2. Ibid.

U.S. Latina/o identities are built through a process of convergence: different stories, different threads come together—only not to erase differences and construct a normative discourse. Instead they come together in order for all the threads to be interwoven, and in order to be sure none of the loose threads have been excluded from the fabric. If we continue to have loose threads, our discourses will be dotted with holes. The silenced voices will break through the holes and dismantle the discourses in order to re-construct the fabric.

Extending this metaphor and applying it to our specific concern, after conversion, U.S. Latina/o Muslims find themselves in one of those holes as a loose thread, as something liminal, in-between. Through the act of re-membering these Muslims can create a new fabric together and restore their thread or part in the fabric. Thus, U.S. Latina/o cultural identities are "very much involved in the cultural and religious dynamics of understanding how the now muted voices of our Iberian forebears, and their lost cultural and religious memories, still touch our hearts and move our minds."[3]

The thread U.S. Latina/o Muslims intend to incorporate into the fabric is one of contested identity. In the same way that medieval Spain was a contested space for multiple identities, today's situation of *latinidad* fits the same model. In this sense, our discourses regarding identity have to be problematized in order to make them more comprehensive and whole: a pluralistic approach to the study of U.S. Latina/o identities. The process of identity construction among U.S. Latina/o Muslims offers a paradigm to address this issue for communities that have been silenced by the normativity of U.S. Latina/o identity. It is developed at three major levels: 1) By looking at the past through a new historical consciousness that allows for the past to be a lived experience; 2) By using cultural memory (the act of re-membering) as a source for self-identification; 3) By looking beyond the normative and colonial representations and breaking through the holes to dismantle the imaginary that supports its construction.

This paradigm certainly does not represent an all-in-all model but it deals with an analysis of contested spaces and contested identities without homogenizing any of them. On the other hand it allows for the convergence of different threads as one constructs U.S. Latina/o identities. What else does this challenge mean for these constructions?

---

3. Hernández, "Hispanic Cultural Identity," 52.

When communities begin to establish an identity as a group, they start by challenging the ideas and stereotypes that have been imposed on them by the dominant culture. As shown in the previous chapter, in the case of U.S. Latina/os, the confrontation takes place not only as they deconstruct the historical narratives that silence their story but also as they re-member those silenced voices and introduce them into a new narrative. The predicament of this process lies in the fact that the stories and voices that make it into the new narratives and identities may then become the norm, and thus leave out or even exclude other voices. The new identities become normative and somehow homogenized, and those whose stories did not make it into the new constructions are left out. The homogenized identity is supported by an imaginary, which guides the images, representations, and discourses that are acceptable.

The presence of the U.S. Latina/o Muslim community in society breaks the heretofore normative aspect of U.S. Latina/o identities, and thus threatens the traditional constructs of culture and identities. These Muslims are forced to demonstrate that their religious transformation does not situate them outside of the U.S. Latina/o community. At the same time, they are also forced to prove to the rest of the Muslim community that they fit in with it, even if their ethnicity is not usually recognized as part of the religious group. This in-betweeness puts U.S. Latina/o Muslims in the complex position of having to explain that while their conversion did indeed transformed them making them different than stereotypical U.S. Latina/os, it did not evaporate their *latinidad*. In other words, their new religious practices and rituals do not change their ethnicities; these U.S. Latina/os do not become what traditionally and stereotypically have been considered culturally Muslim, Arab, or Middle Eastern. And yet U.S. Latina/o Muslims do indeed "go back" and create or retrieve deep connections with the past, and speak of their conversion as part of their cultural tradition. The dis-covery of the cultural memories of a Muslim Spain speaks to both a Muslim and Latino past.

The restoration of this past is not a simple process of finding stories that one can use to prove one's location within a tradition, but a process of "putting together" pieces of a silenced past in order to re-member.[4] At the

---

4. While I have focused my attention on the importance of Muslims traditions in the construction of U.S. Latina/o identities, it is important to acknowledge that the restoring of the medieval history Spain as a source of historical consciousness also applies to U.S. Latina/o Jews, especially (but not limited to) those who have their roots in the tradition of Crypto-Jews in the Southwest. See Golden, *Remnants of Cryto-Jews*.

same time, this act of remembering includes a "historization" of culture in which the foundations of the normative constructions of culture are challenged. The idea of a culture based on a Christian (Catholic) past is deconstructed in order to speak of contested histories and for that matter, contested cultural identities. These contested cultural identities have a past based on contact and exchange, both peaceful and violent. Choosing what aspects of that contact and exchange are most important not only limits the way historical consciousness is constructed but serves as the rationale for deciding who gets left out. For example, the Christian paradigm that dominates most U.S. Latina/o cultural identities' discourses leaves out the Muslim and Jewish voices from Spain, as well as the voices of enslaved Africans.

U.S. Latina/o Muslims engaged in a dis-covery to break these discourses, and this has led to the eventual re-construction of their identities. Now, while these seem to be different projects, in fact they are simply different phases of an extensive project that entails that the convert, in community, be an "engaged" individual in the process. Thus, the product of constructing cultural identities (ever-changing, never fixed) is never delegated to those outside of the community seeking the construction. U.S. Latina/o Muslims begin this project even before conversion through being engaged in a search to find answers to their spiritual anomie. Finding in Islam a place where they fit, they convert, but this decision then places them outside of the traditional cultural understanding of their *latinidad*. In the process searching for a cultural past: 1) they find broken memories; 2) they deconstruct one narrative and create a new narrative based on the dis-covered pasts that build a new consciousness; and 3) they develop a new imaginary based on new cultural memories that lead to new cultural identities.

U.S. Latina/o Muslims, like other U.S Latina/o religious communities, are dependent on cultural memories through which the past is not a discourse but a lived experience that allows for the construction (or re-construction) of identities. Because the act of re-membering is a subversive activity, the epistemic consequence of the identity construction that follows is a direct challenge of the established narratives/discourses that seemed normative. Conversion to Islam may seem to be a subversive activity that tries to subvert the normative conception of *latinidad*, but in actuality it is the process of re-membering the Muslim past that confronts the imaginary. The cultural memories of a Muslim Spain allow U.S.

Latina/o Muslims to locate their conversion as part of the dis-covery of a historical consciousness. As we saw by the examples in the previous chapter, the use of cultural memory offers colonial subjects the opportunity of defining themselves and building a cultural identity grounded in their lived experience.

Other U.S. Latina/o groups who have been left out of the traditional discourses, or who as U.S. Latina/o Muslim have not been included, may follow this particular process, even if it is just one possible pattern and not a rigid formula. Scholars within the fields of U.S. Latina/o religious studies do well to become involved in these discussions rather than re-producing the colonial character of the oppressive systems of power. Opening our discourses means creating decolonized knowledges that facilitate the construction of decolonial identities.

Bibliography

Aidi, Hisham. "Let Us Be Moors: Islam, Race and Connected Histories." *Middle East Report* 229 (Winter 2003). No pages. Online: http://www.merip.org/mer/mer229/229_aidi .html.

————. "Olé to Allah: New York's Latino Muslims." No pages. Online: http://www .beliefnet.com/story/9/story_996.html?rnd=543.

Al-Nasr, Michelle. "A Letter to my Family." *The Latino Muslim Voice* (October-December 2002). No pages. Online: http://www.latinodawah.org/newsletter/oct-dec2k2.html.

Aldama, Arturo J. *Disrupting Savagism: Intersecting Chicana/o, Mexican Immigrant, and Native American Struggles for Self-Representation.* Latin America Otherwise. Durham: Duke University Press, 2001.

Allievi, Stefano. "The Shifting Significance of the *Halal/Haram* Frontier: Narratives on the *Hijab* and Other Issues." In *Women Embracing Islam: Gender and Conversion in the West*, edited by Karin van Nieuwkerk, 120–49. Austin: University of Texas Press, 2006.

Almaguer, Tomás. "At the Crossroads of Race: Latino/a Studies and Race Making in the United States" In *Critical Latin American and Latino Studies*, edited by Juan Poblete, 206–22. Cultural Studies of the Americas 12. Minneapolis: University of Minnesota Press, 2003.

Anzaldúa, Gloria. *Borderlands/La Frontera: The New Mestiza.* San Francisco: Aunt Lute, 1987.

Appiah, Kwame Anthony. *The Ethics of Identity.* Princeton: Princeton University Press, 2005.

Araya Goubet, Guillermo. "The Evolution of Castro's Theories." In *Américo Castro and the Meaning of Spanish Civilization*, edited by José Rubia Barcia and Selma Margaretten, 41–66. Berkeley: University of California Press, 1976.

Arroyo, Edmund A. "A Perspective from Chicago of the Latino Muslim Experience." *The Latino Muslim Voice* (October-December 2002). No pages. Online: http://www .latinodawah.org/newsletter/oct-dec2k2.html#4.

Ashcroft, Bill, et al. *Post-Colonial Studies: The Key Concepts.* Routledge Key Guides. London: Routledge, 2000.

Assmann, Jan. *Religion and Cultural Memory: Ten Studies.* Translated by Rodney Living-stone. Cultural Memory in the Present. Stanford: Stanford University Press, 2006.

Austin-Broos, Diane. "The Anthropology of Conversion: An Introduction." In *The Anthro-pology of Religious Conversion*, edited by Andrew Buckser and Stephen D. Glazier, 1–12. Lanham, MD: Rowman & Littlefield, 2003.

Bal, Mieke. "Introduction." In *Acts of Memory: Cultural Recall in the Present*, edited by Mieke Bal et al., vii–xvii. Hanover: Dartmouth, 1999.

Bibliography

Bender, Thomas. *Community and Social Change in America*. Clarke A. Sanford-Armand G. Erpf Lecture Series on Local Government and Community Life. New Brunswick, NJ: Rutgers University Press, 1978.

Benmayor, Rina, et al. "Claiming Cultural Citizenship in East Harlem: Si Esto Puede Ayudar a la Comunidad Mía . . ." In *Latino Cultural Citizenship: Claiming Identity, Space, and Rights*, ed. William V. Flores and Rina Benmayor, 152–209. Boston: Beacon, 1997.

Bryant, M. Darrol and Christopher Lamb. "Introduction: Conversion: contours of controversy and commitment in a plural world." In *Religious Conversion: Contemporary Practices and Controversies*, edited by Christopher Lamb and M. Darrol Bryant, 1–19. Issues in Contemporary Religion. London: Cassell, 1999.

Cadena, Gilbert R. "Religious Ethnic Identity: A Socio-Religious Portrait of Latinos and Latinas in the Catholic Church." In *Old Masks, New Faces: Religion and Latino Identities*, edited by Anthony M. Stevens-Arroyo and Gilbert R. Cadena, 33–59. PARAL Studies Series 2. New York: Bildner Center for Western Hemisphere Studies, 1995.

Castro, Américo. *The Structure of Spanish History*. Princeton: Princeton University Press, 1954.

———. *Iberoamérica: Su Historia y Su Cultura*. New York: Holt, Rinehart and Winston, 1954.

———. *Origen, Ser y Existir de los Españoles*. Madrid: Taurus Ediciones, 1959.

———. *The Spaniards: An Introduction to Their History*. Berkeley: University of California Press, 1971.

———. *The Spaniards: An Introduction to Their History*. Translated by Willard F. King and Selma Margaretten. Berkeley: University of California Press, 1971.

———. "The Meaning of Spanish Civilization." In *Américo Castro and the Meaning of Spanish Civilization*, edited by José Rubia Barcia and Selma Margaretten, 23–40. Berkeley: University of California Press, 1976.

Conroy, James C. *Betwixt & Between: The Liminal Imagination, Education and Democracy*. Counterpoints 265. New York: Peter Lang, 2004.

De La Torre, Miguel A. "Religion and Power in the Study of Hispanic Religions." In *Rethinking Latino(a) Religion and Identity*, edited by Miguel A. De La Torre and Gastón Espinosa, 286–97. Cleveland: Pilgrim, 2006.

De León, Arnoldo. *They Called Them Greasers: Anglo Attitudes Toward Mexicans in Texas, 1821–1900*. Austin: University of Texas Press, 1983.

Díaz-Quiñones, Arcadio. *La Memoria Rota: Ensayos Sobre Cultura y Política*. Río Piedras, Puerto Rico: Ediciones Huracán, 1993.

Dirlik, Arif. *Postmodernity's Histories: The Past as Legacy and Project*. Lanham, MD: Rowman & Littlefield, 2000.

Durán, Manuel. "Américo Castro y la Identidad de los Españoles." In *Estudios sobre la Obra de Américo Castro*, edited by Pedro Laín Entralgo, 77–91. Madrid: Tauros, 1971.

Dutton, Yasin. "Conversion to Islam: the Qur'ranic paradigm." In *Religious Conversion: Contemporary Practices and Controversies*, edited by Christopher Lamb and M. Darrol Bryant, 151–65. Issues in Contemporary Religion. London: Cassell, 1999.

Eisenstadt, Shmuel N. "The Construction of Collective Identities in Latin America: Beyond the European Nation State Model." In *Constructing Collective Identities and Shaping Public Spheres: Latin American Paths*, edited by Luis Roniger and Mario Sznajder, 245–63. Portland, OR: Sussex Academic, 1998.

Bibliography

Elizondo, Virgilio. "Popular Religion as the Core of Cultural Identity Based on the Mexican American Experience in the United States." In *An Enduring Flame: Studies on Latino Popular Religiosity*, edited by Anthony M. Stevens-Arroyo and Ana María Díaz-Stevens, 113–32. PARAL Studies Series 1. New York: Bildner Center for Western Hemisphere Studies, 1994.

———. *Galilean Journey.* Maryknoll, NY: Orbis, 1983.

Entralgo, Pedro Laín. *Estudios Sobre La Obra De Americo Castro.* Madrid: Taurus Ediciones, 1971.

Fletcher, Richard. *Moorish Spain.* New York: Holt, 1992.

Flores, Juan. "Broken English Memories: Languages of the Trans-Colony." In *Postcolonial Theory and the United States: Race, Ethnicity, and Literature*, edited by Amritjit Singh and Peter Schmidt, 338–48. Jackson: University Press of Mississippi, 2000.

Flores, Richard R. "Para El Niño Dios: Sociability and Commemorative Sentiment in Popular Religious Practice." In *An Enduring Flame: Studies on Latino Popular Religiosity*, edited by Anthony M. Stevens-Arroyo and Ana María Díaz-Stevens, 171–89. PARAL Studies Series 1. New York: Bildner Center for Western Hemisphere Studies, 1994.

Flores, William V. "Epilogue: Citizens vs. Citizenry: Undocumented Immigrants and Latino Cultural Citizenship." In *Latino Cultural Citizenship: Claiming Identity, Space, and Rights*, edited by William V. Flores and Rina Benmayor, 255–77. Boston: Beacon, 1997.

Franco, Jean. "Latin American Intellectuals and Collective Identity." In *Constructing Collective Identities and Shaping Public Spaces: Latin American Paths*, edited by Luis Roniger and Mario Sznajder, 231–41. Portland, OR: Sussex Academic Press, 1998.

Galván, Juan. "Latino Muslims: Leading Others to Enlightenment." *Islamic Horizons* 31:4 (2002) 36–37.

———. "FAQs about Latino Muslims." *The Latino Muslim Voice* (October-December 2002). No pages. Online: http://www.latinodawah.org/newsletter/oct-dec2k2.html.

———. "The importance of Latino Muslim Organizations." *The Latino Muslim Voice* (January-March 2004). No pages. Online: http://www.latinodawah.org/newsletter/jan-mar2k4.html.

———. "Thoughts among Latino Muslims." *The Message International* 30:11/12 (2004) 13–18.

———. "E-Dawah: Fundamentals and Methods." *The Latino Muslim Voice* (April-June 2006). No pages. Online: http://www.latinodawah.org/newsletter/apr-june2k6.html.

———. "Who are Latino Muslims?" *Islamic Horizons* 37:4 (2008) 26–30.

Gillespie, V. Bailey. *The Dynamics of Religious Conversion.* Birmingham, AL: Religious Education, 1991.

Gilliat-Ray, Sophie. "Rediscovering Islam: A Muslim journey of faith." In *Religious Conversion: Contemporary Practices and Controversies*, edited by Christopher Lamb and M. Darrol Bryant, 315–32. Issues in Contemporary Religion. London: Cassell, 1999.

Golden, Gloria. *Remnants of Crypto-Jews Among Hispanic Americans.* Mountain View, CA: Floricanto, 2004.

Gómez-Ruiz, Raúl. *Mozarabs, Hispanics, and the Cross.* Studies in Latino/a Catholicism. Maryknoll, NY: Orbis, 2007.

———. "Ritual and the Construction of Cultural Identity: An Example from Hispanic Liturgy." *Perspectivas* 12 (2008) 9–32.

Bibliography

Gómez, Margarita López. "Mozarabs: An Emblematic Christian Minority in Islamic al-Andalus." In *The Legacy of Muslim Spain*, edited by Salma Khadra Jayyusi, 149–75. Handbuch der orientalistik. Erste Abteilung, Der Nahe und Der Mittelere Osten 12. Leiden: Brill, 1992.

González, Michelle. *Afro-Cuban Theology: Religion, Race, Culture, and Identity*. Gainesville: University Press of Florida, 2006.

Gracia, Jorge J. E. *Hispanic/Latino Identity: A Philosophical Perspective*. Malden, MA: Blackwell, 1999.

Haddad, Yvonne Yazbeck "The Quest for Peace in Submission: Reflections on the Journey of American Women Converts to Islam." In *Women Embracing Islam: Gender and Conversion in the West*, edited by Karin van Nieuwkerk, 19–47. Austin: University of Texas Press, 2006.

Hall, Stuart. "Cultural Identity and Diaspora." In *Contemporary Postcolonial Theory: A Reader*, edited by Padmini Mongia, 110–21. London: Arnold, 1996.

Harvey, L. P. "The Political, Social, and Cultural History of the Moriscos." In *The Legacy of Muslim Spain*, edited by Salma Khadra Jayyusi, 235–58. Erste Abteilung, Der Nahe und Der Mittelere Osten 12. Leiden: Brill, 1992.

———. *Muslims in Spain: 1500–1614*. Chicago: The University of Chicago Press, 2005.

Hernández, Alberto. "Hispanic Cultural Identity and the Recovery of Lost Memory: Response to Raúl Gómez-Ruiz's *Mozarabs, Hispanics, and the Cross*." *Perspectivas* 12 (2008) 41–54.

Hervieu-Léger, Danièle. *Religion as a Chain of Memory*. Translated by Simon Lee. New Brunswick, NJ: Rutgers University Press, 2000.

Holmes, Oliver. Review of *Américo Castro and the Meaning of Spanish Civilization*, by José Rubia Barcia and Selma Margaretten, and *An Idea of History: Selected Essays*, by Américo Castro. *The American Historical Review* 83:4 (1978) 1031.

Isasi-Díaz, Ada María. "A New Mestizaje/Mulatez: Reconceptualizing Difference." In *A Dream Unfinished: Theological Reflections on America from the Margins*, edited by Eleazar S. Fernández, and Fernando F. Segovia, 203–19. Maryknoll, NY: Orbis, 2001.

Jackson, Sherman A. *Islam and the Blackamerican: Looking Toward the Third Resurrection*. New York: Oxford University Press, 2005.

Jawad, Haifaa. "Female Conversion to Islam: The Sufi Paradigm." In *Women Embracing Islam: Gender and Conversion in the West*, edited by Karin van Nieuwkerk, 153–71. Austin: University of Texas Press, 2006.

Jenkins, Chris L. "Islam Luring More Latinos." *Washington Post*, January 7, 2001, C01. Online: http://www.islamfortoday.com/americanlatinos2.htm.

La Shure, Charles. "What is Liminality?" No pages. Online: http://www.liminality.org/about/whatisliminality/.

Lawless, Elaine J. "Rescripting Their Lives and Narratives: Spiritual Life Stories of Pentecostal Women Preachers." *Journal of Feminist Studies in Religion* 7 (1991) 53–71.

López-Baralt, Luce. "The Legacy of Islam in Spanish Literature." In *The Legacy of Muslim Spain*, edited by Salma Khadra Jayyusi, 505–52. Erste Abteilung, Der Nahe und Der Mittelere Osten 12. Leiden: Brill, 1992

López, Yahya 'Abu Ayah.' "What's in a Word." *The Latino Muslim Voice* (July-September 2002). No pages. Online: http://www.latinodawah.org/newsletter/july-sept2k2.html#12.

Machado, Daisy. "Of Borders and Margins: Hispanic Disciples in Texas, 1888–1945." PhD diss., University of Chicago, 1996.

Bibliography

Makki, Mahmoud. "The Political History of al-Andalus." In *The Legacy of Muslim Spain*, edited by Salma Khadra Jayyusi, 3–87. Erste Abteilung, Der Nahe und Der Mittelere Osten 12. Leiden: Brill, 1992.

Martínez-Vázquez, Hjamil A. "*Dis*-covering the Silences: A Postcolonial Critique of U.S. Religious Historiography." In *Nuevas Voces/New Voices: Horizons in US Hispanic/Latino(a) Theology*, edited by Benjamín Valentín, 50–78. Cleveland: Pilgrim, 2003.

———. "Shifting the Discursive Space: A Postcolonial Approach to U.S. Religious History." PhD. diss., Lutheran School of Theology at Chicago, 2003.

Martínez, Juan Francisco. "Origins and Development of Protestantism among Latinos in the Southwestern United States, 1836–1900." PhD diss., Fuller Theological Seminary, 1996.

Menocal, María Rosa. "Al-Andalus and 1492: The Ways of Remembering." In *The Legacy of Muslim Spain*, edited by Salma Khadra Jayyusi, 483–504. Leiden: Brill, 1994.

———. *The Ornament of the World: How Muslims, Jews, and Christians Created a Culture of Tolerance in Medieval Spain*. Boston: Little, Brown, 2002.

Monroe, James T. "The Hispano-Arabic World." In *Américo Castro and the Meaning of Spanish Civilization*, edited by José Rubia Barcia, 69–90. Berkeley: University of California Press, 1976.

Montejano, David. *Anglos and Mexicans in the Making of Texas, 1836–1986*. Austin: University of Texas Press, 1987.

Norris, Rebecca Sachs. "Converting to What? Embodied Culture and the Adoption of New Beliefs." In *The Anthropology of Religious Conversion*, edited by Andrew Buckser and Stephen D. Glazier, 171–82. Lanham, MD: Rowman & Littlefield, 2003.

Parodi, Liliana, et al. "Petition to Protest the Defamation by the Spanish Communication Media Against Muslim Women and Islam." No pages. Online: http://www .petitiononline.com/Muslimah/petition.html.

Parry, Benita. "Problems in Current Theories of Colonial Discourse." *The Post-colonial Studies Reader*, edited by Bill Ashcroft et al., 36–44. New York: Routledge, 1995.

Perry, Mary Elizabeth. *The Handless Maiden: Moriscos and the Politics of Religion in Early Modern Spain*. Jews, Christians, and Muslims from the Ancient to the Modern World. Princeton: Princeton University Press, 2005

Pick, Lucy K. *Conflict and Coexistence: Archbishop Rodrigo and the Muslims and Jews of Medieval Spain*. History, Languages, and Cultures of the Spanish and Portuguese Worlds. Ann Arbor: The University of Michigan Press, 2007.

Quayson, Ato. *Postcolonialism: Theory, Practice or Process?* Cambridge, UK: Polity, 2000.

Rambo, Lewis R. *Understanding Religious Conversion*. New Haven: Yale University Press, 1993.

———. "Anthropology and the Study of Conversion." In *The Anthropology of Religious Conversion*, edited by Andrew Buckser and Stephen D. Glazier, 211–22. Lanham, MD: Rowman & Littlefield, 2003.

Rambo, Lewis R. and Charles E. Farhadian. "Converting: stages of religious change." In *Religious Conversion: Contemporary Practices and Controversies*, edited by Christopher Lamb and M. Darrol Bryant, 23–34. Issues in Contemporary Religion. London: Cassell, 1999.

Recinos, Harold. "Mainline Hispanic Protestantism and Latino Newcomers." In *Protestantes/Protestants: Hispanic Christianity within Mainline Traditions*, edited by David Maldonado, Jr., 194–215. Nashville: Abingdon, 1999.

Bibliography

Reis, João José. *Slave Rebellion in Brazil: The Muslim Uprising of 1835 in Bahia.* Translated by Arthur Brakel. John Hopkins Studies in Atlantic History and Culture. Baltimore: John Hopkins University Press, 1993.

Rikani, Khalil Al-Puerto. "Latino Conversion to Islam: From African-American/Latino Neighbors to Muslim/Latino Global Neighbors." *The Latino Muslim Voice* (April-June 2008). No pages. Online: http://www.latinodawah.org/newsletter/apr-june2k8 .html#3.

Rivera, Khadijah. "Empowering Latino Women." *Islamic Horizons* 31:4 (2002) 37.

Rodríguez, Jeanette, and Ted Fortier. *Cultural Memory: Resistance, Faith, and Identity.* Austin: University of Texas Press, 2007.

Rodríguez, Kenny Yusuf. "Latino Muslims: Islamic Roots of Spanish Culture." *Islamic Horizons* 31:4 (2002) 40–41.

Rodríguez-Puértolas, Julio. "A Comprehensive View of Medieval Spain." In *Américo Castro and the Meaning of Spanish Civilization*, edited by José Rubia Barcia, 113–34. Berkeley: University of California Press, 1976.

Rojas, Raheel. "In Between Religions (Regresa a tu Senior y tu Cultura Latino)." *The Latino Muslim Voice* (April-June 2006). No pages. Online: http://www.latinodawah.org/ newsletter/apr-june2k6.html.

Rosaldo, Renato, and William V. Flores, "Identity, Conflict, and Evolving Latino Communities: Cultural Citizenship in San José, California." In *Latino Cultural Citizenship: Claiming Identity, Space, and Rights*, edited by William V. Flores and Rina Benmayor, 57–96. Boston: Beacon, 1997.

Sánchez, Rosaura. "The history of Chicanas: A Proposal for a Materialist Perspective." In *Between Borders: Essays on Mexicana/Chicana History*, edited by Adelaida R. del Castillo, 1–29. La Mujer Latina Seriers. Encino, CA: Floricanto, 1990.

Sánchez, Samantha. "An Answer: Why Muslim Women Cover." *The Latino Muslim Voice* (July-September 2002). No pages. Online: http://www.latinodawah.org/newsletter/ jul-sept2k2.html.

———. "Islamic Resurgence in Spain and Beyond." *The Latino Muslim Voice* (July-September 2002). No pages. Online: http://www.latinodawah.org/newsletter/jul-sept2k2.html.

Sánchez, Samantha, and Juan Galván. "Latino Muslims: The Changing Face of Islam in America," *Islamic Horizons* 31:4 (2002) 22–30.

Santos García, Mariam. "Musulmanes en la Peninsula Ibérica." *The Latino Muslim Voice* (July-September 2003). No pages. Online: http://www.latinodawah.org/newsletter/ july-sept2k3.html.

Scott, Joan Wallach. *Gender and the Politics of History.* Gender and Culture. New York: Columbia University Press, 1999.

Shohat, Ella. "Notes on the 'Post-Colonial.'" In *Contemporary Postcolonial Theory: A Reader*, edited by Padmini Mongia, 321–34. London: Arnold, 1996.

Silvestrini, Blanca G. "The World We Enter When Claiming Rights: Latinos and Their Quest for Culture." In *Latino Cultural Citizenship: Claiming Identity, Space, and Rights*, edited by William V. Flores and Rina Benmayor, 39–53. Boston: Beacon, 1997.

Sturken, Marita. "Narratives of Recovery: Repressed Memory as Cultural Memory." In *Acts of Memory: Cultural Recall in the Present*, edited by Mieke Bal, Jonathan Crewe, and Leo Spitzer, 231–48. Hanover: University Press of New England, 1999.

Bibliography

Taylor, Donald. "Conversion: inward, outward, and awkward." In *Religious Conversion: Contemporary Practices and Controversies*, edited by Christopher Lamb and M. Darrol Bryant, 35–50. Issues in Contemporary Religion. London: Cassell, 1999.

Tweed, Thomas A. *Our Lady of the Exile: Diasporic Religion at a Cuban Catholic Shrine in Miami*. Religion in America Series. New York: Oxford University Press, 1997.

van Nieuwkerk, Karin. "Gender and Conversion to Islam in the West." In *Women Embracing Islam: Gender and Conversion in the West*, edited by Karin van Nieuwkerk, 1–16. Austin: University of Texas Press, 2006.

———. "Gender, Conversion, and Islam: A Comparison of Online and Offline Conversion Narratives." In *Women Embracing Islam: Gender and Conversion in the West*, edited by Karin van Nieuwkerk, 95–119. Austin: University of Texas Press, 2006.

Vásquez, Manuel A. "Rethinking *Mestizaje*." In *Rethinking Latino(a) Religion and Identity*, edited by Miguel A. De La Torre and Gastón Espinosa, 129–57. Cleveland: Pilgrim, 2006.

Viscidi, Lisa. "Latino Muslims a Growing Presence in America." *Washington Report on Middle East Affairs*, June 2003, 56 and 58. Online: http://www.wrmea.com/archives/june2003/0306056.html.

Weber, David J. *Myth and the History of the Hispanic Southwest: Essays*. The Calvin P. Horn Lectures in Western History and Culture. Albuquerque: University of New Mexico, 1988.

Zaid, Saraji Umm. "Latinos, Islam, and New York City." *The Latino Muslim Voice* (January–March 2002). No pages. Online: http://www.latinodawah.org/newsletter/jan-mar2k2.html#9.

———. "Latinos Eager for Islam." *Islamic Horizons* 31:4 (2002) 30.

Index